TAKING IT SERIOUSLY

Taking it Seriously

A Faith Leader's Guide to Domestic Violence

GENEECE GOERTZEN

Foreword by Jay Kieve

CASCADE *Books* • Eugene, Oregon

TAKING IT SERIOUSLY
A Faith Leader's Guide to Domestic Violence

Copyright © 2024 Geneece Goertzen. All rights reserved. Except for brief quotations in critical publications or reviews, no part of this book may be reproduced in any manner without prior written permission from the publisher. Write: Permissions, Wipf and Stock Publishers, 199 W. 8th Ave., Suite 3, Eugene, OR 97401.

Cascade Books
An Imprint of Wipf and Stock Publishers
199 W. 8th Ave., Suite 3
Eugene, OR 97401

www.wipfandstock.com

PAPERBACK ISBN: 978-1-6667-7791-8
HARDCOVER ISBN: 978-1-6667-7792-5
EBOOK ISBN: 978-1-6667-7793-2

Cataloguing-in-Publication data:

Names: Goertzen, Geneece, author. | Jay Kieve, foreword.

Title: Taking it Seriously : A Faith Leader's Guide to Domestic Violence / Geneece Goertzen; foreword by Jay Kieve.

Description: Eugene, OR: Cascade Books, 2024 | Includes bibliographical references and index.

Identifiers: ISBN 978-1-6667-7791-8 (paperback) | ISBN 978-1-6667-7792-5 (hardcover) | ISBN 978-1-6667-7793-2 (ebook)

Subjects: LCSH: Family violence—Prevention. | Spouse abuse—Prevention. | Spirituality.

Classification: HV662 G655 2024 (paperback) | HV662 (ebook)

07/05/24

Duluth Power and Control Wheels, used with the permission of:
DOMESTIC ABUSE INTERVENTION PROGRAMS
202 East Superior Street, Duluth, Minnesota 55802
218-722-2781 | www.theduluthmodel.org

Experience of Harm Assessment, used with the permission of:
www.santolinaconsulting.com

Dedication

To the many survivors with whom I have had the honor of speaking, whose fortitude and tenacity are clearly evident despite numerous challenges . . . you are my heroes.

To the family, friends, and colleagues who encouraged me to write and provided conversation and feedback along the way, and to those who took part in previewing early versions of this book . . . you are my strength.

To my extraordinary children who were my reason to escape our own lengthy and devastating story of abuse, and who inspired my journey to healing . . . you are my treasures.

To the dearest one who taught me that true love does exist, who has treated me with kindness and respect, considered me an equal, supported my pursuits, and celebrated my accomplishments . . . you are my bliss.

To God who liberated me from bondage, who sustained me and called me to this ministry, and who provided beauty for ashes . . . you are my hope and peace.

People concerned with the kingdom of God will be people concerned with justice.
—Rev. Hannah Coe

Contents

Foreword by Jay Kieve		ix
Abbreviations List		xi
Introduction		xiii
1	Domestic Violence Basics	1
2	Victim Case Study	8
3	Forms of Domestic Violence	15
4	Power and Control Are the Root of Abuse	22
5	Patterns of Abuse	26
6	Dynamics of Healthy and Toxic Relationships	30
7	Who Are These Victims of Domestic Violence?	38
8	The Abuser Is Not Your Average Congregant	44
9	Consistent Conflict, It Really Is That Bad	49
10	Spiritual Weariness Runs Deep	54
11	Why Victims Might Stay in the Abuse	59
12	Domestic Violence and Marriage	65
13	Domestic Violence and Divorce	72
14	Preaching, Teaching, and Training Leadership	78
15	Women in Ministry and Church Leadership Are Vital in the Response to Abuse	84
16	How to Respond to Domestic Violence	89
17	Helping Survivors Find Healing	96

CONTENTS

18	Why It Matters and Putting It All into Practice	101
19	Back to the Victim Case Study	107
Alphabetical Glossary of Domestic Violence Terms		109
Appendix A: Resources		141
Appendix B: Church Policy Template and Checklist		143
Appendix C: Premarital Counseling		147
Appendix D: Ways to Recognize Abuse		149
Appendix E: How to Assess Change in Perpetrators		152
Bibliography		157

Foreword

WHEN HAGAR WAS PREGNANT and ran away from Sarai's violence in Gen 16, the angel of the Lord met her with comfort and a promise. She named the Divine One "the God who sees" because God acknowledged her plight and offered her hope. Later, in Gen 21, when Sarah forces Hagar from her home again, now with young Ishmael in tow, she finds herself in a desperate situation. Having lost hope and given up Ishmael to death, she is again met by the angel of God. In this second scene, God has heard the cries of the child and provided for the pair water that saves their lives. God's seeing and hearing Hagar's experience of a violent home led to actions that brought hope, life, and future prosperity.

Tragically, millions of people suffer domestic violence in invisibility and silence while in the company of people of faith. According to the Centers for Disease Control's *National Intimate Partner and Sexual Violence Survey*, almost one in two women and more than two in five men suffered at least one impact from contact sexual violence, physical violence, or stalking by an intimate partner.[1] About 115 million people reported suffering psychological violence perpetrated by their significant other.[2] The absence of victims or survivors of domestic abuse in a congregational gathering would constitute a statistical anomaly. Yet, few pastors address intimate partner violence from the pulpit, and seldom is information about protective shelters or supportive services prominently displayed.

---

1. Leemis et al., *National Intimate Partner and Sexual Violence Survey*, 5.
2. Leemis et al., *National Intimate Partner and Sexual Violence Survey*, 6.

FOREWORD

With *Taking It Seriously: A Faith Leader's Guide to Domestic Violence*, the Reverend Geneece Goertzen seeks to equip ministers and lay leaders with the tools to see, hear, and respond to victims and survivors of intimate partner violence. Informed by her careful research as both a minister and a social worker, Rev. Goertzen offers helpful perspectives on the experiences of people living with domestic violence who seek support from their faith and faith leaders. She then provides church leaders with ideas and resources carefully and faithfully to support survivors in their midst.

Faith leaders who engage *Taking It Seriously* will first learn the basics of domestic violence, including the various forms of violence, how power and control form the nexus of abuse, and how victims experience loss of agency that leads to entrapment in toxic relationship. Building on the information that helps leaders recognize abuse, she then turns her attention to the experiences of victims at church. Clergy discover how messages about marriage and divorce, purity, and gender roles impact victims both positively and negatively. Rev. Goertzen provides helpful insight into the ways theological expression and church practice might be shaped to support help and healing for people experiencing domestic violence. Finally, she provides a glossary, resource links, policy recommendations, and a primer for premarital consultation that can form the basis for discussing and planning a faith community's response to domestic violence.

For people of faith who follow the God who sees, hears, and responds with hope and life, closing our collective senses to the experiences of people who are abused should no longer be an option. *Taking It Seriously: A Faith Leader's Guide to Domestic Violence* creates an informed invitation to support victims of intimate partner violence that clergy and lay leaders can follow as they faithfully follow their God. Equipped with Rev. Goertzen's research and recommendations, faith leaders and their congregations can be a source of hope and life for the victims who are surely a part of their community.

REV. DR. JAY KIEVE
Director of Ministerial Transitions, Abuse Prevention and Response Advocate, Cooperative Baptist Fellowship

Abbreviations List

CC&DV	"Congregations, Clergy, and Domestic Violence"
CDC	Centers for Disease Control and Prevention
DAIP	Duluth Domestic Abuse Intervention Programs
DARVO	Deny, Attack, and Reverse Victim/Offender
DV	Domestic Violence
IPV	Intimate Partner Violence
NCADV	National Coalition against Domestic Violence
UN	United Nations

Introduction

THIS BOOK IS A culmination of my personal lived experience as a survivor of more than two decades of domestic violence, years of speaking with victims and survivors of abuse, continuous reading and study on this topic, involvement with domestic violence organizations, and formal divinity and social work education. Together, these contribute to the creation of my voice and proficiency on this topic, as I pursue a PhD with the intent of continuing to advocate for awareness and improved response to domestic violence.

For the health and well-being of congregants, the church must confront domestic violence and respond with compassion and support. To not respond appropriately is to allow the oppression to continue. Maybe cases of domestic violence are increasing, or maybe abuse is just more visible. What victims hid in previous generations is more obvious now because people are daring to speak up regarding a topic that many churches haven't reckoned with yet.

You will find that I use the words *victim* and *survivor* throughout this book. Often *victim* describes someone still in the abuse, while *survivor* describes someone who has left the abuse, which is how this book will use the terms, although other literature may use them interchangeably. Please note that this book will not describe every situation of domestic violence or provide answers to every question. The nuances of a particular case will require that you integrate what you learn in this book with what you see before you to provide care for those in need.

The book shares a mixed-methods research project I created while completing my masters-level education. The research focused on faith leaders' training, beliefs, comfort levels, and practices regarding domestic violence, as well as interviews with survivors about disclosing the abuse they experienced to their pastors and churches. As survivors shared, it was evident that there was a need for additional assistance. This replicated findings in prior research, showing the necessity for church preparedness, congregational care, and pastoral support.

This book aims to be exactly that—a domestic violence guide and glossary for increasing education and awareness among clergy members and faith leaders, including those serving in lay leadership positions. The unique domestic violence glossary got its start when I was in graduate school, and I have continued to expand and revise it, describing terms and including suggestions for those serving in faith-based spaces. The language and terminology used by victims and survivors may be unfamiliar, and even common words can present differently in a domestic violence context. The glossary contains the words in bold throughout this book.

I want to include a trigger, or content, warning here for those who may pick up this book after having experienced abuse themselves. Resilience and recovery take time. It is an ongoing process that shows bravery, strength, and intentionality. Please care for yourself as needed throughout the book. I appreciate your willingness to help others who are experiencing the same.

To all my readers, on behalf of the many victims and survivors who desire domestic violence education and awareness for their faith leaders and churches, thank you for reading and engaging with this topic. Thank you for seeking to respond faithfully and desiring to create a faith community conducive to safety and healing. Thank you for caring.

1

Domestic Violence Basics

DOMESTIC VIOLENCE IS A pattern of behaviors used to gain and maintain **power and control** over another person in an intimate relationship.[1] The National Coalition against Domestic Violence includes willful intimidation and threats in its definition.[2] The CDC defines intimate partner violence (IPV) as abuse or aggression between partners in a romantic relationship, which includes physical or sexual violence, psychological aggression, and **stalking**.[3] Domestiv violence (DV) or IPV can be a single episode or last for years, or even decades. Acts of abuse do not need to always be physically violent. Mind games, verbal tirades, financial or spiritual control, and neglect are also forms of DV and IPV.

In the 1990s, the term *domestic abuse* became common as it is more inclusive of mental and emotional manipulation and threats.[4] Gender-based violence, battering, and spousal abuse are additional terms to describe violence between partners in a relationship. Family violence describes abuse among those residing in the same household, whether intimate partners or not. **Dating**

---

1. Hotline, "Understand Relationship Abuse," para. 3.
2. See NCADV, "Statistics."
3. CDC, "About Intimate Partner Violence," 1.
4. Collins, *Out of Control*, 2.

violence is the term used for abuse in couples who are not married. Domestic violence is a form of **elder abuse** in senior couples. Domestic violence has even been called intimate partner terrorism, which, for those who are familiar with the insidious nature of **coercive control**, is not a term without merit. Because DV is a term widely familiar in the United States, it is the one used in this book.

Every minute, twenty-four individuals are subject to physical violence, rape, or stalking by an intimate partner, affecting millions of people each year.[5] Survivors of abuse are twice as likely to develop symptoms of depression, three times more likely to develop an anxiety disorder, and three times more likely to meet the criteria for post-traumatic stress disorder (PTSD).[6] The United Nations states that for women of childbearing age, gendered violence causes as many deaths as cancer and as much disability as road accidents and malaria combined.[7] According to the United Nations Office on Drugs and Crime, the home is the most dangerous place for women, as it is the location where most intimate partner homicides occur at the rate of six per hour around the globe.[8]

According to a 2022 CDC report, the lifetime prevalence of physical violence, stalking, or contact sexual violence by an intimate partner is over 47 percent for women and 44 percent for men.[9] The same report indicated that psychological aggression was over 49 percent for women and 45 percent for men.[10] Other reports will show varied but similar findings, depending on the specifics of what was being measured, the entity performing the surveys, and the year of the study. It is important to note that counting the situational instances of aggression mentioned above

---

5. Hotline, "Domestic Violence Statistics," under "General Domestic Violence Statistics."
6. Hotline, "Domestic Violence Statistics," under "Mental Health Statistics."
7. UN News, "Staggering One-in-Three," para. 1.
8. Office on Drugs and Crime, "Home," para. 1.
9. Leemis et al., *National Intimate Partner and Sexual Violence Survey*, 4.
10. Leemis et al., *National Intimate Partner and Sexual Violence Survey*, 6.

does not include other forms of DV, nor does it consider the more gendered nature of coercive control. Multiple studies have shown that ongoing and underlying patterns of denigration, intimidation, exploitation, isolation, and domination that induce fear of harm are overwhelmingly used by men against women.[11]

Most first-time victimization occurs prior to the age of twenty-five.[12] Domestic violence affects all ethnicities, education levels, societal classes, genders, and ages. The incidence of physical violence, stalking, and rape by an intimate partner is even higher among non-white individuals.[13] Those in any historically marginalized community are at greater risk for victimization. **Intersectionality** demonstrates how those with multiple factors, including age, class, ethnicity, and gender, can intersect and increase risk. Domestic violence is not an accident. It is an intentional choice made by one individual seeking to control another. Alcohol, drug use, anger, stress, and anxiety can make the situation worse but do not cause abuse.

Because DV is generally not a single episode, but rather the repetitive use of abusive tactics targeted against an individual, or even an entire family, it becomes the typical pattern of interaction within the household. Partners learn to attempt to regulate and adjust to toxicity, and children grow up having to navigate unhealthy attitudes and behaviors, much to the family's detriment. Abuse often grows worse over time, increasing in frequency and intensity.

The tactics of abuse can vary throughout the life of the relationship, depending on the perpetrator's desire for control in any particular situation. The following graphic illustrates how abuse can create varying levels of harm. One victim may experience lower levels in some areas and higher levels in others. Some victims may not experience abuse in every area, while still others may experience high levels in each of the areas.

---

11. Myhill, "Measuring Coercive Control," 357.
12. Leemis et al., *National Intimate Partner and Sexual Violence Survey*, 8.
13. Leemis et al., *National Intimate Partner and Sexual Violence Survey*, 7.

Taking it Seriously

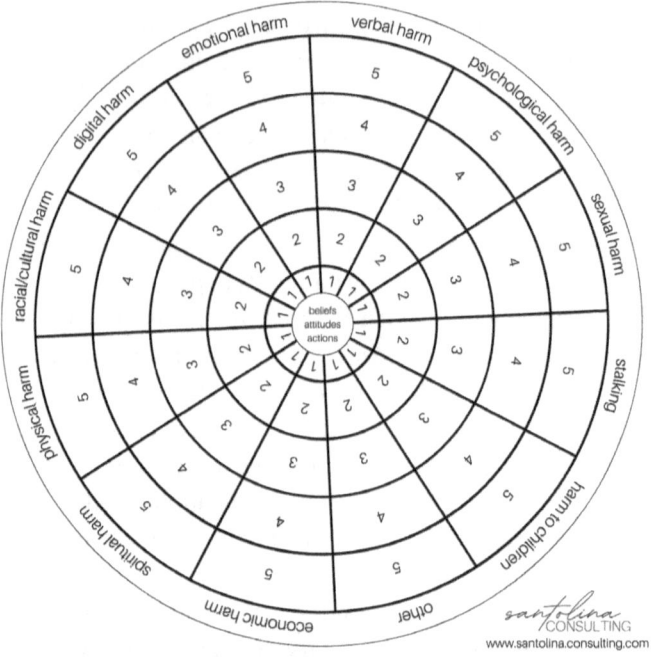

Figure 1[14]

It is vital that faith leaders fully comprehend that religious households are not exempt. The statistics illuminating abuse in religious homes echo those in nonreligious homes.[15] Religion can be a means of comfort to those who are abused, but can also increase risks for harm.[16] Women of faith are more likely to conceal the DV they experience and are less likely to leave an abusive marriage.[17] They also tend to use religious language when explaining their tolerance of abusive marriages.[18] Religious beliefs strongly influence

---

14. Holsomback, "Experience of Harm Assessment."
15. Westenberg, "When She Calls for Help," 2.
16. McMullin et al., "When Violence Hits," 114.
17. Nason-Clark et al., *Religion and Intimate Partner Violence*, 30.
18. Westenberg, "When She Calls for Help," 3.

their decisions about staying in the abuse, even when danger is present.[19]

Negative health outcomes such as depression, PTSD, digestive and nervous disorders, chronic pain, heart conditions, and other physical and mental health issues are linked to DV for adults and children.[20] Domestic violence has a profound and widespread impact on families. This is not an adult-only problem. Empirical studies found that the presence of DV increases the risk of child abuse (physical, psychological, or neglect), with a co-occurrence rate of 30–60 percent.[21] Research indicates that children witness up to 90 percent of the abuse that occurs at home.[22] Witnessing DV has the same negative impacts as experiencing it.[23]

Childhood domestic abuse deeply affects the children who witness and/or experience it. Childhood **trauma** impacts behavior, as well as both mental and physical health in children and youth. The church has a role in preventing and intervening in cases of abuse. Childhood exposure to abuse and societal attitudes that deny the occurrence and minimize the effects of abuse are the primary reasons that DV continues to be a problem in our nation. A consistent link exists between men who experienced abuse as children and those who abuse their partners.[24] The impact on families makes informing and educating our faith communities a vital task. Abuse has no place in any home. To protect our children and break the transmission of violence between generations, faith leaders must confront and respond to DV.

Clergy are often the first contact for a victim of abuse who needs assistance.[25] Even women who are not religious may reach out to a church for assistance with an abusive relationship.[26] In fact,

---

19. McMullin et al., "When Violence Hits," 114.
20. CDC, "About Child Abuse and Neglect."
21. Zolotor et al., "Intimate Partner Violence," 318.
22. Hamby et al., "Children's Exposure," 1.
23. Office on Women's Health, "Effects of Domestic Violence on Children."
24. Nason-Clark et al., *Religion and Intimate Partner Violence*, 9.
25. Perilla, "Role of Churches," 1.
26. Shannon-Lewy and Dull, "Response of Christian Clergy," 655.

more than 75 percent of survivors will share the abuse they have experienced with an informal support person, including friends, family, or a clergy member.[27] Churches are in a unique position to help the hurting. Congregations are a valuable potential support for victims and survivors of DV, and faith leaders have an opportunity to correct harmful theology, encourage healthy behavior in relationships, and assist victims and survivors.

However, multiple studies have shown that many pastors feel inadequately equipped to effectively respond to abuse,[28] and faith leaders have acknowledged the need for greater DV training and resources for both prevention and intervention.[29] Unless you are particularly astute regarding all individuals in your congregation, and unless you fully understand the tactics of abuse, the ways in which it is minimized, and how trauma manifests in children, it wouldn't be hard for someone without training to miss the signs of DV. When spiritual abuse is part of the issue, as it tends to be in religious homes, it leaves victims feeling as if God has willed this abuse in their lives, or that God isn't concerned about the ways in which their spouses harm them.

As leaders in congregations or ministries in which our faith informs our practice, we have an obligation to create change. Many of the psalms declare that God cares about the oppressed, attends to their suffering, and binds their wounds. The Bible is also clear that God does not condone harmful acts. Wicked hearts plot violence (Prov 24:1–2). Not keeping a tight rein on one's tongue renders a person's religion worthless (Jas 1:26). Not providing for those in one's household is equated to denying the faith (1 Tim 5:8). Indeed, we are to do good to all, especially to those in the household of faith.

Creating change requires effort. It requires bravery. It requires that individuals and groups be willing to call out wrongdoing and stand up for victims and survivors of abuse. Domestic violence

---

27. Houston-Kolnik et al., "Overcoming the 'Holy Hush,'" 135.

28. Homiak and Singletary, "Family Violence in Congregations," 25–26; Zust et al., "10-Year Study."

29. Houston-Kolnik et al., "Overcoming the 'Holy Hush,'" 147.

thrives in silence and shatters families. Unless we break the silence and oppose abusive behavior, it will continue to destroy future generations. One of my seminary professors said that maybe pastors don't respond well because they don't understand that DV exists in their congregations. This book seeks to revolutionize that narrative and equip anyone serving in churches and faith-based institutions to actively implement transformation within their spheres of influence. It is my hope that you will take this seriously. This is the work of the people of God.

2

Victim Case Study

KELLI WAS A SINGLE mom when she met Dalton. She was working full-time and attending college full-time. She was a diligent employee who enjoyed her job, and the store promoted her to department manager after a year. She was also a conscientious student who enjoyed her college classes and excelled in most of them. She sought to make a good life for her child, but being a single parent was often challenging, especially with little support from family or friends. She started attending church at the invitation of a college classmate, and there she met Dalton. She thought that meeting someone at church was a good thing.

He seemed quite enamored with her, which flattered her lonely soul, and he soon involved himself in every aspect of her life. On occasion he would randomly show up at her place of employment, which felt awkward; but he said he just wanted to see her. He questioned her about work, school, and church acquaintances, which felt invasive; but he would say that he was just trying to protect her and that she needed to be careful about who was in her life. No one had ever told her about the differences between concern and control, so she didn't recognize the behavioral **red flags**. Amazingly he seemed to like everything she liked, which almost felt too good to be true. What she wanted for her future was everything he claimed he wanted in his. On the surface, this seemed amazing, but she had never heard of **mirroring** and **future faking**.

It was a whirlwind romance, and he promised the world. The pressures of single parenting, work, and going to school made it feel like she needed what he promised. He pressured her to get married right away, so she agreed. Almost immediately things began to change. On the honeymoon, he started talking about his interest in having sex with other people. Within the first month of marriage, he claimed that the church where they met was not a true example of godliness and that it was not proper for her to be in a college classroom with male professors. They stopped going to church and he required that she drop out of college.

He was insistent about his role as head of the household. Growing up, she had heard that men were to be the authority of the home, so she felt it was inappropriate to speak up. He usurped the savings she had so carefully acquired and maxed out her credit card on purchases that he said were necessary for their apartment. Within months she was pregnant, and he convinced her that it would be better if she just quit her job to stay home with the kids. Much to her dismay, she now had no church, job, or financial resources of her own, in addition to the abruptly ended college education she had been so proud of. It turned out that he pretty much didn't like anyone, so it was rare that they got together with other people.

Kelli sought to find contentment in her new life because she believed that was the Christian thing to do. She looked for joy in each new day and poured herself into homemaking because he said that housework and childcare were not his responsibility. He had chosen an apartment that was above their means, and now several months into the marriage he started to blame her for quitting work and not contributing to the household funds. She attempted to remind him that it was his idea for her to stop working, but he didn't want to hear about it and insisted his recall of the events was the right one. She learned quickly not to even try to reason with him because he refused to listen and would start to yell.

She began to doubt her ability to think clearly due to the consistent confusion. The concept of **gaslighting** was unfamiliar. He told her that he knew multiple forms of martial arts, how he had previously injured those who dared to double-cross him, and that his former associations with dangerous characters and illicit jobs had prepared him for all he needed in life. He had never shared any of this before they were married. Was he making it up, or was he telling the truth? He would tell stories with great specificity, only to later say it was all in **jest** and she should just lighten up, but then he would threaten that she must never share his **secrets**.

When she was seven months pregnant, he required that she go to the local indoor range to watch him practice shooting his new gun, despite knowing she was afraid of guns. They had only one vehicle, a little car her parents had given her when she started college. Bothered by the fact that his name wasn't on the title and using the excuse that they were about to have a baby, he traded her car in for one he liked better—something he knew she didn't like at all. He took their one vehicle to work, leaving her at home with young children and no transportation.

He gave away her favorite things, saying they created clutter, but was always buying himself expensive gadgets and starting costly new hobbies. He took out loans on her good credit due to some issue with his own credit that he said was the fault of someone else. They moved into a small house in a rural town where they knew no one, and where they were miles and miles away from grocery stores and medical care. He wouldn't allow her to plant anything in the yard because he claimed she had a black thumb and would kill it, and that she was just doing it to get the neighbors' attention, but he started an orchard and then let it rot. If dinner wasn't to his liking, he threw it across the room and made her clean it up.

He mortified her by claiming that if she wore shorts or pants it was an invitation for other men to look at her, so she switched to long, shapeless dresses. His assertions seemed a bit absurd considering how painfully shy she had always been, but since she didn't often leave the house, it probably didn't matter much how she dressed. He terrified her with his reckless driving. His

mood swings were frequent. When he was mad, he destroyed things and ranted about the house projects he had started but never finished, as if somehow that was her fault. And yet, if the phone rang, he could be instantly jovial with the person on the other end of the line.

He lectured her about her lack of accomplishments. He criticized her appearance, even though she was following his orders. He regularly tried to force her to view pornography and would threaten to rape her when she refused. He claimed that the Bible required that she do anything and everything he said, immediately when he said it, and that she needed to be more submissive to his leadership. He made a lot of claims about the Bible for someone who said he hated church and couldn't quote a single Bible verse correctly. She stayed quiet to keep the peace.

Dalton became cold and domineering and never had a kind word for anyone. He was constantly irritable, had a dreadful temper, and would often engage in screaming and lecturing that lasted for hours. When he was away from the house, he constantly called to check up on her. Kelli truly tried to make the best of it. She dedicated herself to making it work and prayed for peace in the home. She tried to convince herself that she could make him happy and put sincere effort into doing so. She kept the house sparkling clean because he was upset by the slightest mess, even though he actually made those messes himself.

The Christian marriage books she read claimed that prayer and submission were the answer to marital difficulties. They made her feel that the abuse was her fault, or at least her problem until the end of time because marriage was forever. Every breath became a pleading for strength, and every prayer sought God's mercy to make it through the day. It hadn't always been this bad. It was easier earlier in the marriage, but over time the consistency and force of the aggression grew. The former reprieves, especially after the larger outbursts, were fewer and farther between.

There were frequent indications of affairs, but she tried to put that out of her mind. After all, he said that she was lucky to have him because anyone else would have thought that a single mom was a stupid, f—ing whore. She didn't think of her marriage as abusive because the physical abuse was minimal at first. Those marriage books didn't describe abuse and didn't discuss sexual assault. He told her that because they were married it wasn't rape and that no cop and no court would ever hold it against him. She feared he was right and told no one, but there really wasn't anyone she could tell anyway.

No one knew what she lived with, not even family. She felt so alone because she was so very alone. Although he often talked about leaving her, he said that if she ever tried to leave him that she would never see the kids again. The children were her one joy. She couldn't imagine life without them. She feared what he might do to them if she weren't there to absorb his outbursts herself. Recently, in a fit of rage, he had thrown her across the room. She knew better than to even shed a tear because he would say that she was seeking pity.

When she looked in the mirror, she no longer recognized herself. Her eyes were hollow, her smile was gone, and her shoulders were slumped. She went through her days almost like a robot, going through the motions mechanically in the order they were supposed to occur. The constant turmoil had left her just an empty shell of the quiet but cheerful girl she once was.

How had it come to this? Dalton turned out to be nothing like the person he had appeared to be. This was not the life she anticipated. It baffled Kelli. She was doing everything she could to make things better. Despite years of intense prayer and Scripture meditation, it was getting worse. In fact, as she tried to cheerfully submit, he became even harsher and more vicious. He often threatened to kill her and slept with a gun under his pillow. She would literally shake incessantly as she tried to fall asleep at night. Her entire being was exhausted, and she was afraid for the kids. Her faith had held her together to this point, but she needed a miracle.

WHAT CAN WE LEARN FROM THIS CASE STUDY?

Case studies help us understand and recognize the ongoing, insidious nature of abuse. As you read through the various types and tactics of DV in the next chapter, you will identify the forms of abuse and control that are present in this case study. Although physical abuse was not always present, it did increase over time. Fear of harm was enough to keep her in line. Sexual assault was frequent. Financial abuse existed in multiple ways. Frequent surveillance was present via calls and texts. He wouldn't let her attend church, except on rare occasion when he went with her. He harassed her both day and night, and verbal aggression was incessant. He had isolated them in a small rural town where no one could suspect what they lived with, no DV services were available, and he was buddies with the part-time police officer. The excessive emotional and verbal abuse had taken a toll on her body, soul, and spirit. Continued submission gave him full control over every aspect of her life. Kelli assumed that abuse was defined only as severe physical assault and did not realize the danger she was in. Without education and information about abuse and a support system to help her, things were not likely to change.

Using the "Experience of Harm" graphic introduced in the previous chapter, we can visually describe Kelli's marriage when she realized she needed a miracle. Multiple forms of abuse were very high. The *other* category for this case is used to represent neglect. Overall, Dalton was quite negligent, really only caring about his own needs and wants. Regarding the children, there was a lot of yelling and screaming in the house, he made choices that put the family at risk, and his carelessness with finances was evident, but she had never seen him hit the kids. Dalton wasn't particularly adept at technology so stalking and digital harm were present but less so than they might have been if he were technologically savvy. They were not from a historically marginalized group, so the racial/cultural category didn't apply in this case study.

An observer might fill out an illustrated graphic like this differently than a survivor would. An adolescent in a home where domestic violence is present might fill it out differently than the victimized parent. The victim might assess the situation a bit differently while still in the abuse than once out of the abuse with more education about the nature of how DV affects those within the home. The essential point of this chapter and this case study is to connect you with an authentic example of what DV victims face and how their lives are completely changed and consumed by experiences of abuse. Such examples serve to enlarge empathy, provide insight, and further acquaint you with the world of DV advocacy and awareness.

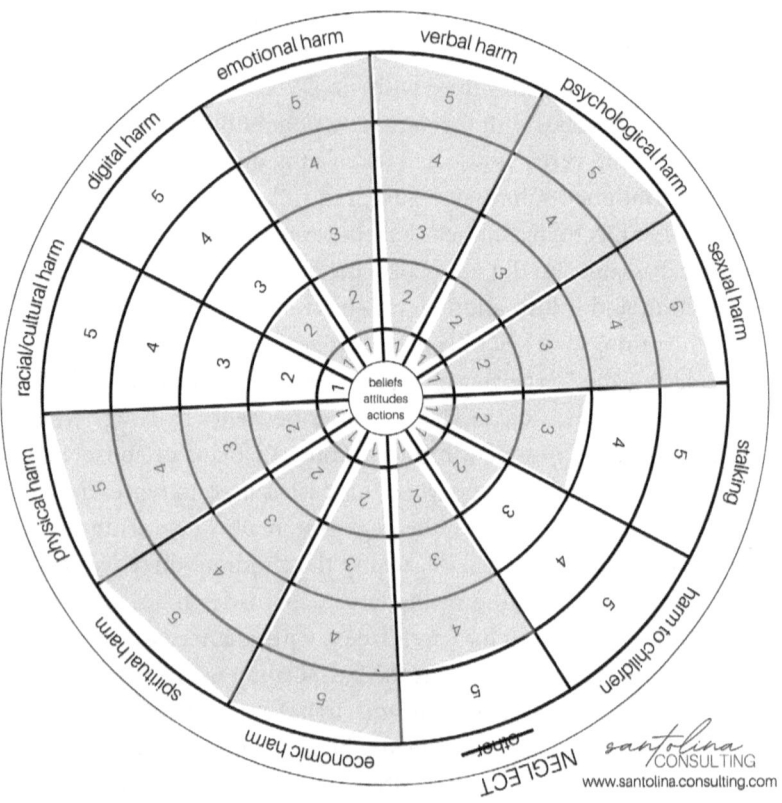

Figure 2[1]

---

1. Holsomback, "Experience of Harm Assessment."

3

Forms of Domestic Violence

Abuse exists in many forms, and in most cases, multiple types of abuse will coexist in the same relationship creating a tangled web through tactics of control. Varying attitudes and behaviors, from mild to severe, will appear over the course of unhealthy or abusive marriages. A victim does not have to check a long list of boxes for a relationship to be toxic.

The lists below are representative of the ways abuse can exist in a relationship. Please understand that these lists are not exhaustive. Abuse can and does exist in other forms. And sometimes a form of abuse will cross over into multiple categories, for example, threats or body-shaming can be both emotional and verbal abuse.

PHYSICAL ABUSE

- Damaging household items, walls, or property
- Pushing, shoving
- Slapping, hitting, punching
- Pulling hair
- Biting
- Burning

- Strangulation (choking)
- Forced drug or alcohol use
- Use of weapons, or the threat of the use of weapons
- Driving recklessly
- Pushing the victim out of a moving car
- Abandoning the victim in an unknown or dangerous place
- Locking the victim out of the house
- Throwing things at the victim (even if it misses)
- Sleep deprivation
- Disfigurement
- Physical restraint
- Homicide/murder
- Harming pets, or threatening to harm pets

EMOTIONAL OR PSYCHOLOGICAL ABUSE

- Isolation
- Intimidation
- Dominance
- Threats
- Blackmail
- Manipulation
- Guilt, shame
- Taunting
- Bullying
- Anger, angry posture, or hostile facial expressions
- Creating fear of harm through a fascination with weapons
- Creating an unsafe emotional environment

FORMS OF DOMESTIC VIOLENCE

- Consistent violation of boundaries
- Jealous/possessive behavior
- Expecting the victim to ask permission
- Blame shifting, or asserting that everything is the victim's fault
- Creating a catastrophe out of something that isn't
- Public embarrassment
- Ridiculing vulnerability and tenderness
- Baiting the victim to get a response
- Gaslighting—causing victims to doubt their sanity
- Controlling all major decisions
- Eliminating systems of support

VERBAL ABUSE

- Yelling, screaming
- Swearing
- Name-calling
- Body-shaming
- Insults, criticism
- Humiliation
- Lecturing
- False accusations
- Aggressive or violent language
- Belittling accomplishments
- Sarcasm or humor at the expense of the victim
- Accusations used to turn the children against the other parent
- Threats to the victim, or threatening friends/family of the victim

SEXUAL ABUSE

- Rape, sexual assault, forced sex (even in marriage)
- Manipulation into sex acts that the victim doesn't want
- Unwanted touching
- Unwanted sexting
- Coerced sex against doctor's orders (after childbirth or surgery)
- Sexual duty; expecting that a partner always be available sexually
- Demanding sex after other forms of abuse
- Reproductive coercion or sabotaging the use of contraceptives
- Forced pregnancy
- Forced abortion
- Miscarriage due to violence
- Accusations that the victim is cheating
- Blaming the spouse for one's own affair or pornography use
- Forced pornography use
- Having an affair as revenge or manipulation
- Trafficking or forced prostitution

ECONOMIC ABUSE OR FINANCIAL ABUSE

- Controlling how family finances are spent
- Taking the victim's paycheck, inheritance, or disability payments
- Not allowing the victim access to money
- Making the victim beg or perform favors for money
- Not allowing the victim to work
- Preventing the victim from having transportation to work
- Forcing the victim to work

FORMS OF DOMESTIC VIOLENCE

- Harassing the victim at work
- Not allowing the victim opportunities for advancement
- Not putting the victim's name on accounts, vehicles, or housing
- Forced filing of fraudulent financial documents
- Forging the victim's signature
- Coerced debt; secretly taking out loans in the spouse's name
- Destroying the victim's credit
- Refusing to be financially responsible
- Using family finances on gambling or running up credit card debt

DIGITAL OR ELECTRONIC ABUSE

- Excessive calling, texting, or checking up to control and harass
- Using technology to track or monitor the victim
- Setting up video cameras to increase surveillance
- Using smart home features against the victim
- Requiring the victim's passwords
- Oversight of online activity
- Using media to harass or stalk
- Posting insulting or humiliating content about the victim
- Pretending to be the victim on social media
- Not allowing access to any form of media/social media
- Revenge porn; unauthorized sharing of intimate images

SPIRITUAL OR RELIGIOUS ABUSE

- Using religious ideology to control or keep the partner in line
- Twisting Scripture to reinforce attitudes and behaviors

- Misinterpreting Scripture to enforce rigid gender roles
- Censorship based on perceived scriptural authority
- Denying the victim the ability to make personal spiritual decisions
- Not allowing the victim to attend faith services
- Requiring a particular church or version of the Scriptures
- Requiring the victim to adhere to certain religious ideals
- Requiring certain clothing based on religious ideals
- Using religion to guilt or shame the victim
- Creating penalties for any perceived sin
- Using the church or religious authorities against the victim

NEGLECT AS ABUSE

- Withholding affection
- Silent treatment
- Refusing to take responsibility
- Never offering approval or affirmation
- Not providing medical, dental, or mental health care
- Not supplying adequate clothing, food, or shelter
- Not providing a safe home environment
- Abandonment

POST-SEPARATION ABUSE (ANY ABUSE THAT CONTINUES AFTER SEPARATION/DIVORCE)

- Stalking, tracking, and use of technology to monitor
- Harassment
- Revenge

FORMS OF DOMESTIC VIOLENCE

- Pressure, bullying, creating fear of harm
- Excessive filings/litigation through the court system
- Putting the children at risk
- Using the children against the other parent
- Undermining the other person's influence on the children
- Withholding child support payments
- Not supplying court-ordered insurance or reimbursements
- Refusing to consent to children's activities or medical care/therapy
- Getting other adults to abuse the victim (abuse by proxy)

4

Power and Control Are the Root of Abuse

THE DULUTH DOMESTIC ABUSE Intervention Programs (DAIP) in Duluth, Minnesota, developed the Power and Control Wheel along with the Equality Wheel, seen at the end of this chapter, as tools for education and abuse intervention.[1] The Power and Control Wheel depicts abuse, sustained through tactics of power and control in the relationship. Physical and sexual violence are visible on the outer rim of the wheel, and some forms of control are evident between the spokes of the wheel. Other forms of abuse not shown on the wheel do exist, especially in marginalized populations. DAIP has multiple adaptations of these wheels for specific applications and communities.[2] In contrast, the Equality Wheel shows how nonviolent, **healthy relationships** exist through attitudes and behaviors rooted in equality.

In our case study example, besides the physical and sexual violence, Dalton utilized the tactics of abuse in each spoke of the wheel. As you read through the text in the spokes, think back to the ways he intimidated Kelli, played mind games, isolated her,

1. Domestic Abuse Intervention Programs, "Understanding the Power and Control Wheel."
2. Domestic Abuse Intervention Programs, "Wheel Library."

blamed her, threatened to take the children, used male privilege, limited her access to finances, and used coercion and threats. There was no portion of the Power and Control Wheel not reflected in their relationship. In contrast, regarding the Equality Wheel, there was no aspect of safety, respect, supporting her goals in life, honest and open communication, shared parenting or responsibility, economic partnership, or negotiation in their relationship.

Another way to discuss abusive behaviors is by defining them as overt or covert. Overt abuse is visible, explicit, and observable. It is what many people tend to think of when they consider domestic violence–related behaviors. Covert abuse is less apparent, especially to people outside the relationship, and controls the victim through hidden, underhanded means. Annette Oltmans, founder of the Mend Project, explains it this way, "Overt behavior is more obvious, therefore it's harder to miss, while covert behavior can be difficult to detect, identify, and describe."[3]

The term coercive control describes the use of these tactics in a relationship. Coercive control limits freedom and traps an individual in a relationship, producing social, emotional, and financial barriers to escape.[4] For women of faith, it creates spiritual barriers as well. With coercive control, many victims don't recognize the abuse, just like Kelli in our case study example. The high presence of covert abuse tactics with a lower incidence of overt abuse can leave victims feeling distressed and confused about what they are experiencing.

You can show these wheels to individuals when discussing the possibilities of abuse to see how they describe their relationships. Does their relationship look more like the Power and Control Wheel, or like the Equality Wheel? The Equality Wheel displays what we want to see in a relationship, where the foundations are trust, respect, and honesty—attitudes and behaviors that reflect Christian living. You can learn more about these in appendix A and visit the Duluth website to print or purchase copies, including wheels in other languages. Their website features additional

3. Mend Project, personal communication regarding "Overt vs. Covert."
4. Dichter et al., "Coercive Control," 597.

adaptations showing power/control and equality in a Christian home or church environment, as well as many others.

Figure 3[5]

---

5. "Power and Control Wheel," in Domestic Abuse Intervention Programs, "Wheel Library."

POWER AND CONTROL ARE THE ROOT OF ABUSE

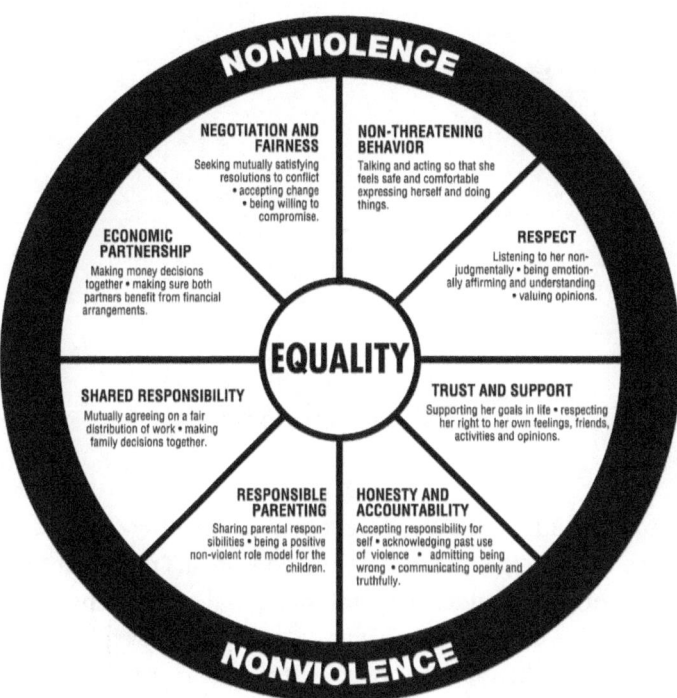

Figure 4[6]

6. "Equality Wheel," in Domestic Abuse Intervention Programs, "Wheel Library."

5

Patterns of Abuse

LENORE WALKER FIRST DESCRIBED and defined the *cycle of abuse* in 1979 at the beginning of the battered woman's movement.[1] Her research provided evidence for this cycle, and many **domestic violence service providers** continue to use it. Abusive patterns are described in a three-phase cycle. First is a tension-building phase in which conflict grows and victims often amend and adjust their behavior to calm their partner and keep things from escalating. Next is an acute explosion (or battering) phase with aggression, outbursts, or other forms of abusive behavior. It ends with a **reconciliation** or kindness phase where the abuser may express remorse or offer excuses to gain sympathy for the explosion.

Some victims describe cycles that happen rapidly, and others describe slow-moving ones that rotate over weeks and months. Smaller cycles of nonviolent abuse may rotate within larger cycles of more drastic abusive behaviors, creating chronic tension. The perpetrator may use gifts, affection, and elaborate promises to pull the victim back into the relationship, a tactic known among DV advocates as **hoovering**. During the reconciliation phase (also known as the honeymoon phase), most victims believe that the proclamations of regret or apology are sincere. In this phase, their

---

1. Walker, *Battered Woman*, loc. 115.

abuser more closely resembles the person they fell in love with, and less like the one who threatened and harmed them during the explosion. In their desire for life to return to happier times, victims may pardon abusive behavior and try again to make things work.

In the reconciliation phase, victims are less likely to press charges against their abuser or may recant previous accusations. Religious women are more likely to think that the change is real and will last.[2] What is usually lacking in the reconciliation phase, however, is sincerity in the apologies and a genuine admission of responsibility for the abuse. It is hard for victims, and even outsiders, to see the manipulation and lack of contrition when they have little knowledge about the nature and tactics of abusive behavior.

Most victims eventually realize after years of abuse that the behavior displayed during the reconciliation phase is simply a ruse—a manipulative effort cloaked in manufactured kindness meant to bring them back under the control of the abuser. Feigned remorse tends to work because it recreates **hope** for the victim. In difficult times, hope anchors their souls. Hope that this time things will be better. Hope that this time the change is sincere. However, as these cycles of **false repentance** continue to repeat, hope diminishes and optimism fades.

There are some who describe DV as more of a roller coaster with increasing intensity than a cycle. Some describe waves of abuse, rather than cycles. There are others who assert that the language of the battered woman syndrome perpetuates dominant gender roles and is not adequate to describe non-white and other minority responses.[3] Certainly progress over time has provided women more ability and agency to speak up rather than stay silent. The point here is not to argue about models and frameworks. Whichever model you choose to use, it is important to understand that abuse is not stagnant. It is ever present and ongoing, even when things appear to be calm. Also, even though DV tends to have patterns, this doesn't mean the victim can predict when it will happen or how bad it will get.

2. Nason-Clark, *Religion and Intimate Partner Violence*, 1.
3. Sokoloff, *Domestic Violence at the Margins*, 194–99.

Taking it Seriously

According to DV expert Lundy Bancroft, experiencing physical aggression is abuse, even if it happens only once.[4] That is true for other forms of abuse as well. When the perpetrator realizes that there are few consequences for toxic behavior, the abuse will escalate. Small incidents of abuse in the first months and years of marriage will increase over time. Sometimes decades of marriage have elapsed before the victim can clear the fog of the confusing behavior to name it for what it really is. This is what happened with Kelli in our case study. Based on the marriage materials that she read, Kelli felt she wasn't allowed to speak to others about how she was treated, and that praying for him was her only option.

Do not blame a victim for staying, especially because the victim may be intensely hoping that this time the promises made in the reconciliation phase will be real. Religious and societal pressures to stay and make things work mean that many victims remain in the abuse longer than they would stay if they had tangible support from these sectors. It can be dangerous for clergy members to send a victim back home, **minimizing the abuse** because "everyone yells" or "it was barely a slap." DV is so much more than meets the eye.

Many clergy members underestimate the prevalence and severity of DV.[5] This can affect how they counsel victims and survivors. Likewise, it is generally unwise to confront the abuser or to force the victim to leave the relationship. Either of those could make the situation more dangerous for the one experiencing the abuse. It also removes autonomy from victims to make decisions based on their unique situations. Victims are the experts of their own lives, and we must support them as they seek to protect themselves and their children.

It is within a faith leader's role to become aware and educated about abuse, to provide resources and referrals, and to have a relationship with the local family violence shelter. For churches without a local shelter, having a connection to a licensed **trauma-informed** counselor, a state organization that provides a

---

4. Bancroft, *Why Does He Do That*, 128.
5. Tracy, "Clergy Responses to Domestic Violence," 10.

victim-centered approach to caregiving, or the family violence unit at the police or sheriff's station is an alternative. Church leadership can also address church policies regarding abuse and make sure there is an atmosphere of support for victims and survivors and an intolerance for all forms of abusive behavior.

In the case study example of Kelli and Dalton, Kelli noticed that the abuse occurred in cycles long before she ever heard of the cycle of abuse. After a verbal or physical explosion, Dalton seemed to be calmer and easier to talk to again. For a few hours, days, or weeks if she were fortunate, things seemed more like what she remembered before they married. In the early years, she could laugh again and didn't feel that he would attack her at any moment, although in later years laughter was nonexistent and fear was always present. Then the tension would begin to rise again. In this tension-building phase, she had to be very careful about everything she said or did because anything could set him off at any moment, without much rhyme or reason.

Kelli called this **walking on eggshells**—a term described in the glossary section of this book. Then, without provocation, an incident of abuse would occur, whether it be verbal, emotional, sexual, or physical. In the reconciliation phase, there were sometimes excuses for the abuse, but more often it was as if it never occurred. Dalton would simply act as if everything were normal. Certainly, there was never an apology. Kelli expected apologies in the beginning because she believed that is what someone should do after showing poor behavior, but she quickly learned that it was better to not expect an apology than to wait for one that never came.

6

Dynamics of Healthy and Toxic Relationships

KNOWING ABOUT HEALTHY AND **toxic relationships** is really the beginning of understanding how abuse manifests within such relationships. What may look like someone's personality quirks or behavioral oddities may, in fact, be harmful patterns that injure and oppress others. Toxic behavior patterns lead to abuse when not held in check and corrected. Homes of origin (even religious ones) may have modeled injurious behavior, which causes individuals to repeat the cycle of what they believe to be normal household interactions.

Abusive individuals have misguided, entitled ideas about their rights and privileges in the home that cause them to justify these toxic behaviors against their families. This can be especially true in cases of strict **gender role expectations** where men are always in charge and women must be obedient to them. When left unchallenged, gender bias becomes ingrained in culture as a structural norm, rather than acknowledged as a violation of a woman's human rights.[1] This is true in the church as well. When religious institutions do not address this bias, some men believe they have a right to mistreat their wives. Verbal, emotional, financial, spiritual,

---

1. Thomas and Beasley, "Domestic Violence as a Human Rights Issue," 39.

sexual, and physical abuse or neglect become patterns of behavior to assert dominance in the relationship.

Due to this tendency, faith leaders and religious institutions need to speak up about these unjust biases and practices. Philip Payne, the author of *The Bible vs. Biblical Womanhood*, digs deep into the original language and cultural context of New Testament passages often used to control women. He states that the Bible clearly shows that the Christian home has no room for harshness, and submission is to be mutual between the partners.[2] These are vital insights because when hierarchy and headship are misunderstood or misrepresented by faith communities and abusive partners, women can feel that they must continue to tolerate the abuse.

Women have shared that in some faith communities, there are implications or even explicit statements that they cannot speak out about abuse because doing so would demonstrate gossip and a lack of submission in the home. This ideology excuses abusive behavior and forces victims to stay silent. When faith leaders do not specifically denounce all forms of abusive behavior, they unwittingly side with those who perpetuate DV against their families. We must be willing to clearly state that abusive behavior is never okay. There is no excuse for it. Perpetrators must take full responsibility for their own behavior. Victims are not at fault.

I truly believe that pastors, leaders, and teachers in faith communities must discuss relationship dynamics at all age levels. The church can teach children about healthy relationships in the context of bullying, bodily autonomy, friendship, and kindness to others. The church should state that physical and psychological aggression is never acceptable. That can graduate into a discussion about healthy versus unhealthy dating relationships in youth groups where red flags, **green flags**, stalking, and **grooming** techniques like **love bombing** are defined and described. Again, the discussions of bullying and bodily autonomy are a good introduction to the concept of inappropriate behavior between individuals, using those discussions to draw parallels with unhealthy behavior in the context of dating.

---

2. Payne, *Bible vs. Biblical Womanhood*, loc. 2296.

Taking it Seriously

It is much easier to have these conversations before individuals are emotionally invested in a relationship. Young adults need this information before they get married because it is easier to address abuse before marriage than after. Premarital counseling should include discussions of how to identify unhealthy behavior patterns, the various forms of abuse, and how to get help if needed. Doing this during premarital counseling sets the expectation that abusive conduct is always wrong. It also provides a connection back to the pastor if abuse ever occurs in the relationship. If talking about abuse during the engagement feels uncomfortable for the couple or for the pastor, know that it will not get any easier after the wedding. See appendix C for more discussion of premarital counseling.

As I prepared this book and had conversations with members of the clergy, it was encouraging to hear that several were planning to start including DV in their premarital counseling sessions. I trust that they will, in turn, discuss this with other pastors of their acquaintance and that this will be more common in the future. Discussing DV in premarital counseling does not guarantee that an already abusive relationship will end immediately, but it does put supportive structures in place.

There is a chance that by the time a couple gets to premarital counseling, toxic attitudes and harmful actions will already be normalized in the relationship. Between the excitement of wedding planning and the victim's belief that everything will be okay, or thoughts that one partner can love the other into being a better person, it may be hard to make adjustments in the premarital counseling sessions. **Fear tactics** may already be in place to keep the victim in line.

Marriage does not end or solve unhealthy behavior patterns but rather brings them to the forefront, just as they did for Kelli in our case study example. Getting married quickly, as Kelli and Dalton did, means there isn't time to decipher confusing tendencies or realize that the real person is hiding behind a mask of artificial virtue. Concealed, overlooked, or unrecognized behavioral red flags become clear as the wedding and honeymoon excitement wears off.

Many victims and survivors have explained to me that their new spouse literally turned abusive the day they were married, as if the ceremonial permanence meant he no longer had to control himself, or that his oppressive behavior was now legitimized by a marriage certificate. A marriage ceremony does not grant a person license to begin to harm a spouse, to act without respect, to use coercive control and violence, or to assert themselves as the sole authority. Philip Payne writes that the apostle Paul does not describe headship and hierarchy in marriage, but rather an equality between spouses.[3]

I have also heard that there is an assumption that marriage and children will help a restless man settle down. The opposite is usually true. As already stated, abuse tends to get worse after the wedding. It also tends to increase during pregnancy. Abuse during pregnancy leads to complications and poor outcomes for both mothers and babies.[4] Pregnancy also increases the risk of DV-related homicide, which is a leading cause of death in pregnant women.[5] In cases where spousal abuse exists, child abuse often exists as well,[6] and at a rate fifteen times higher than average.[7]

Talking about abuse with adults in their middle-aged years is important because a spouse's poor behavior may become more toxic, the abuse may become more frequent, or maybe a congregant's adult child is in an abusive relationship and needs help. Even senior adults need these conversations as **gray divorce** trends grow and the reasons older adults decide to divorce come to light. Keep in mind that abuse in senior adults may be subject to mandated reporting in your state.

Truly, these discussions are essential at every level of interaction with congregants, and having these conversations regularly communicates your knowledge and willingness to engage with difficult topics. Multiple participants interviewed for my research

---

3. Payne, *Bible vs. Biblical Womanhood*, loc. 1035.
4. Modi et al., "Role of Violence," 254.
5. Wallace, "Trends in Pregnancy," 1333.
6. Zolotor et al., "Intimate Partner Violence," 316.
7. Martin, "This April, Let's Talk," cutout.

stated that their church was not aware of the signs of abuse, pastors were not equipped to help, and there were never any conversations or sermons about what healthy and toxic relationships looked like. Education and awareness for faith leaders, as is contained in this book, can change that.

As you have these dialogues, include age-appropriate discussions of **consent** in all of them. Whether the conversation is about bullying, cybercrimes, dating violence, DV, or clergy sexual assault, knowing about consent is vital for all ages and genders. If you are already having conversations about grooming and cyberstalking to keep your youth safe, it would be natural to also include additional information about consent within relationships.

Everyone needs to know how to define consent. Everyone needs to agree to respect the **boundaries** of others, in all contexts of friendship and relationships. Everyone needs to know that *no* is a complete sentence, and that silence does not indicate consent. Understanding consent and boundaries promotes autonomy and equality in relationships, which is exactly what we want to endorse with all age levels and groups inside our faith communities.

Talking about healthy relationships can help sort out what is harmful in communication with spouses, which can lead to helpful conversations about improving relationships. Counseling can help couples with minor difficulties improve communication or deal with bad habits before things get worse. Healthy relationships allow for freedom in conversation or actions without fear of consequences. If a congregant is afraid of a spouse, it would be prudent to learn more about why there is fear. Also, keep in mind that fear is subjective. If someone shares legitimate fears with you, do not dismiss them just because you wouldn't fear the same thing. There is no way for you to know the patterns of behavior used to create that anxiety and apprehension. Appendix D may be of help in recognizing abuse.

The example of marital disagreements is helpful here. In a healthy relationship, a couple will manage differences with cooperative conversation about ideas, thoughts, feelings, and possible outcomes. They can settle arguments fairly easily when both are willing to take responsibility and apologize for any wrongdoing. In a healthy relationship, one spouse does not dread voicing a disagreement and does not panic over retaliation when expressing an opinion. Neither fears a conversation, and there is no grand challenge with one spouse desiring to cut the other down and win at all costs.

In my master's level research titled "Congregations, Clergy, and Domestic Violence" (CC&DV), 47 percent of faith leaders believed that it was somewhat important that the couple talk through the conflict, and 28 percent believed that it was very important. The remaining 25 percent of responding faith leaders felt that it was not important to have the couple talk through the conflict. However, talking things out will not create harmony in an abusive relationship. It will not fix the marriage. Interestingly, statistical analysis of these responses found that fewer women than men believed that talking through the conflict was important, and younger faith leaders were less likely to view it as important than older faith leaders (defined as age sixty and older).[8]

Where toxicity exists, differences of opinion and arguments are situations in which one spouse becomes fearful of the other over time. A perpetrator can use any form of abuse to create fear or harm, including weaponizing the victim's faith. The victimized spouse learns that it is often safer to just let the toxic spouse win. This is the desired outcome for perpetrators because it increases their control in the home. They take no responsibility for injury and offer no true apologies. If ever the perpetrator concedes, it is held against the victim and becomes yet another point of contention. It is essential that we are aware of these details because it changes how we approach handling these situations in the church.

If it comes to your attention that DV exists in a relationship, **couples counseling** is no longer a safe choice. Although many pastors recommend marriage counseling in cases of abuse, it is difficult to do so safely.[9] First, DV is not a mutual problem. Abuse is not a situation where you can encourage cooperation between spouses,

8. Goertzen and Fox, "Response of Christian Faith."
9. Rotunda et al., "Clergy Response," 363–64.

because the ones perpetrating abuse will generally not see that they have any fault in the relationship. Second, the victim needs to have a safe space to share experiences, away from the abusive spouse. In a couples counseling session where any form of abuse exists, the perpetrating partner may dominate the session, blame the victim, or not allow the victim to freely speak about any concerns.

If the victim should dare to speak of any problems or specifically mention abuse in a joint counseling session, that victim is in danger of further intimidation, retaliation, and abuse after leaving that counseling session. Additionally, it is possible for a counselor to underestimate the seriousness of the abuse when the abuser does not display blatantly abusive tendencies during the counseling session. Perpetrators will usually refrain from using violence, aggression, and intimidation tactics when there are witnesses, particularly witnesses they can gain as allies, or manipulate into **triangulation**.

My interviews with survivors revealed that religious ideology kept them and their children in abusive homes. Several had their churches counsel them to stay in abusive marriages, and the abuse continued or even worsened. Historically many victims have had no choice but to remain in abusive marriages, largely due to religious teachings and national law, although, it is interesting to note that divorce was not unheard of in the Puritan colonies, including for desertion, absence, cruelty, and failure to provide.[10]

In some faith communities, female obedience and submission are common topics. Some speak of negative circumstances and judgment from God due to a wife's disobedience. Victims and survivors described to me not just messages of submission via intimidation from the pulpit, but the fact that this intimidation happened in the name of God. Men have privileges in society and churches that women do not, and recognizing how this affects relationship dynamics within the families in our congregations means that we are more informed when trying to help.

Whether serving in an official church capacity or as a lay leader, we must all defend the wounded, protect children, and join

---

10. Baskerville, "Puritan View of Divorce."

the cause to end abuse. Discussing healthy and toxic relationships is not a single discussion, but rather many conversations over months and years. Churches, clergy, chaplains, counselors, and lay leaders in faith communities should welcome discussions about healthy and toxic behavior and see them as essential in their congregations. How pastors understand and define DV is an important part of that. The earlier section outlining the many forms of abuse and how they appear in relationships needs to be common knowledge among faith leaders so that it is referenced and shared regularly.

Through my CC&DV research, I asked faith leaders how they defined DV. It was encouraging to see that most respondents included each of these forms of abuse in their definition: physical, sexual, emotional, verbal, financial, stalking, and neglect. However, many of my conversations with victims and survivors indicated that their clergy had a very narrow definition of DV, often limiting it to just some forms of physical assault. There is no way to know about those particular differences in my research because that information wasn't my focus. Based on the survivor interviews, it is likely that those speaking out about their disappointing experiences are coming from congregations that are less informed about abuse or more inclined to use doctrines of submission and marriage permanence.

It is not hard for churches to be informed about abuse. Information about DV is readily available from a variety of sources, and there are many **advocates** who would be willing to assist where needed. Check with those in your congregation who may have training. Seek out the local family violence shelter or DV advocacy group. Attend DV conferences and seminars. Read books and listen to podcasts on abuse prevention and survivor support. Do an internet search. Talk to survivors about their experiences. As you become more educated and aware of the dynamics of abuse and how it afflicts those who experience it, your empathy will grow and your capacity to faithfully assist those harmed by DV will increase. You will understand why we need to take this seriously.

7

Who Are These Victims of Domestic Violence?

THERE ARE MISCONCEPTIONS THAT victims are undereducated, dependent, financially unstable, or have personalities that cause or attract abuse. These misconceptions may include ideas about race, lack of religion, or disadvantaged backgrounds. The truth is that sometimes the victim of abuse is the person you'd least expect. Many victims are experts at keeping up appearances and hiding what they live with each day. They have learned to make the best of a bad situation. I have known victims with doctoral degrees and others who are financially set or successful by society's standards. I have talked with many, many victims and survivors who had a strong Christian upbringing and believed they were marrying a person of faith and solid character. Yet, these individuals found themselves in abusive marriages.

It can be hard to believe that abusers target victims, but it is true. In the context of DV with people of faith, abusers will exploit the victim's religious devotion, empathetic nature, and desire to please. Perpetrators of abuse often believe that their victims belong to them and may use the bonds of marriage, or quote Scripture, to support the idea of ownership. The spouse perpetrating the abuse may pretend to be an engaged member of a congregation or even hold a position of leadership in a church. This person may exude perfection and holiness at church, and then subject the family to severe abuse when there are no witnesses. No one knows what happens at home because many victims stay silent due to the **shame** that often accompanies abuse.

Victims often feel that they cannot speak freely about what they live with, and sometimes the abuser threatens them to keep quiet. If they do speak of their experiences, it may be a sanitized version of what is going on. Many victims do not recognize it as abuse at first. They may instead refer to a spouse's behavior as confusing, difficult, or stubborn. These words paired with warning signs of abuse are an indication that faith leaders should pay close attention. The illustration of an iceberg is useful here. The victim shares just a small part of what goes on in the home, with most of the evidence hidden beneath the surface. However, if victims receive a safe and supportive **church response**, they will feel secure enough to disclose more.

Rigid power structures in toxic homes may demand unquestioning obedience. The male abuser may regard his victim as a subservient domestic slave married for his personal gain. A female victim must do the cooking, cleaning, and childbearing without complaint, and often without help from the abuser who feels no need to engage in tasks he considers beneath him. Some abusers expect their victims to provide elaborate meals and perfectly tidy homes without the finances or tools to accomplish these tasks. Some victims do not have free access to money or a vehicle to obtain adequate food, clothing, or medical care for themselves and their children.

In the case where the abusive spouse is female, she may express harsh demands, be impulsive and display jealousy, not allow her spouse to have friends or outside interests, or simply refuse to contribute to the household. I know a male survivor of abuse who worked a full day and then came home to cook, clean, and care for the kids because his wife refused to do so. The male survivors I spoke with felt that a pastor wouldn't believe that their spouse caused them harm.

Taking it Seriously

Some survivors that I have spoken to say their spouse expressed interest in their faith prior to the marriage, only to express disinterest or even mock them for it after the wedding. These victims go into the marriage believing they are equally yoked to one who has claimed to be a committed follower of Jesus, only to realize the cruel deception after the wedding. Such a situation is not unlike false advertising—promising one thing but delivering another. It is the bait-and-switch routine of an unscrupulous salesperson. Yet in marriage, particularly in the church, we cannot return the faulty item. Instead, these victims believe that they have no options, especially when faith leaders speak of marriage as eternal and divorce as a failure.

I assure you that victims and survivors of DV are some of the most forgiving, patient, and long-suffering people that I have encountered. By the time the situation comes to the attention of the clergy, a chaplain, or even a volunteer in a faith-based organization, they have endured months or years of verbal, emotional, and/or physical harm. They tried to make it work. They are tired. And wounded. And brokenhearted. Their spouses have manipulated their goodwill and compassion for nefarious purposes.

The survivors interviewed for the CC&DV research, both women and men, were from a variety of Christian denominations and a range of church sizes. Most were dedicated to their faith and their churches. Few of their spouses showed continued interest in the church after the wedding, although a couple of the perpetrators were well-regarded leaders in the congregation.

Despite the survivors' dedication to their churches, the majority did not receive support from their churches once they disclosed the abuse. Instead, they were on the receiving end of unhelpful comments and hurtful actions. One was blamed for the abuse, one was shunned, and another had a pastor ask what she could do to save the marriage. One church kicked a victim out of her small group. Another said the church supported her abuser over her even with clear evidence of his appalling misconduct. Faith leaders told these women to pray, be more submissive, reconcile with the abuser, or simply responded with no response at all.

WHO ARE THESE VICTIMS OF DOMESTIC VIOLENCE?

Victims devoted to their faith may cling to their relationship despite the abuse. A victim may think that prayer, Bible study, or submissive behavior will eliminate the abuse, especially if a pastor or faith leader makes these claims. Some Christian marriage books, speakers, and social media influencers have perpetuated this myth, along with **minimizing** the reality of the abuse by reducing it to nothing more than petty conflict or errors in communication. And yet, as stated earlier, abuse is not a minor marital issue in which both partners contribute equally to the problem. Domestic violence is willful contempt and intentional harm by one partner against the other.

Statistics show that women are more often the victims of DV, sustain more serious injuries, and have higher lifetime costs related to intimate partner violence.[1] Victims will often underreport or trivialize the abuse, make excuses for the spouse, and blame themselves; while the abuser is often self-righteous, justifies behavior, blames others, and shows little compassion. Men can strike intense and deadly terror into their victims, in a way that communicates that they mean business, especially if enamored with weapons. While men can be victims of abuse, they do not tend to fear their wives in the same ways that women may fear their husbands. Women who use defensive force may do so in reaction to violence or to prevent an impending attack.[2] If it comes to your attention that the victim has exploded, consider the context. Incessant **baiting** and provoking could elicit a defensive reaction.

If someone comes to you for help with their troubled or confusing relationship, know that DV may be involved. Know that abuse happens even in couples that appear happy and engaged in the church. Know that perpetrators can be people you really like, and victims can be the people you'd least expect. Start by meeting individually with each of them. If one of the partners is reluctant to do that, consider that to be a possible indication for concern. Perpetrators usually won't want a faith leader alone

---

1. CDC, "About Intimate Partner Violence," 2.
2. Miller, *Journeys*, loc. 363.

with their victim, and victims may be afraid of their abuser's response to such a meeting.

Sometimes the perpetrator projects a pitiful image by **playing the victim**. In the DV advocacy world, this may be described with the acronym **DARVO**, because the accused will engage in denying, attacking, and reversing the roles of victim and offender. I have heard countless examples of this scenario from women who described how their abusive spouses went to their pastors to accuse them of being the abusive person in the relationship. If you are unsure about who is the victim in the marriage, start with the list of signs of abuse at the beginning of this book and consider the dynamics of the relationship.

It is helpful to determine which individual has power and influence. Is there an established hierarchy in the home that would cause an imbalance of power? Who is demanding their rights? Who is showing genuine humility? Does one deny everything and blame the other? Is one launching an attack on the other's character? Who has the prestige or financial status to render their spouse unable to fight a bitter divorce process or lengthy custody battle? Does one spouse have a more prominent family? Who or what is involved in each individual's support network? Is one being displaced from the church family due to leaving the abuse? Which spouse has more to lose? Does one partner have limited access to finances? Has one been a stay-at-home parent with limited education and work experience? If there are children in the relationship, who is trying to protect them, and who is using the children as a pawn?

Don't just listen to the accusations of the more verbal and assertive partner. The partner holding power and abusing the other will often use **projection** to discredit the victim and attempt to get others to misplace fault in the relationship. Survivors described how they were blamed for the exact things the perpetrator did, including drug use and affairs. If one partner is acting like a spoiled toddler throwing a tantrum, you may be looking at the perpetrator. A victim often displays confusion, anxiety, worry, fear, and weariness. A victim may minimize harm, be nervous about intervention, and engage in self-blame. But that is not always the case. Sometimes the actual abuser is eerily calm and emotionless while behind the scenes taunting and provoking the victim into a state of discomposure. There is no single stereotype.

If you are still unsure, pray for discernment, and get the help of a DV expert at your local DV support program or through state and national DV coalitions. Check appendix A for more information about where to find resources. It should be a general principle that a church operates first in the interests of victims. God's care for the oppressed supports this ideal. Jesus' examples of advocating for the wounded, the hurting, the outcast, and the downtrodden encourage care for those victimized by abuse. A church shows courage, strength, and compassion when it stands with victims and survivors of DV. Be willing to take a step back, slow down, and listen with humility.

Remember that abuse escalates and intensifies over time. Keep in mind that exposure even to just one or two forms of abuse can be soul-crushing and deeply hurtful. Victims of toxic and abusive behavior may struggle to recover due to a lack of support, including a lack of concern from their faith communities. As part of the healing process, survivors need you to listen to them without bias, to recognize their pain, and to believe their experiences of harm. Your knowledge of abuse will create a helpful and supportive environment that is conducive to healing. Your willingness to take this seriously will go a long way toward supporting **resilience** in those who have been harmed by DV.

8

The Abuser Is Not Your Average Congregant

Few people truly understand the viciousness of DV, and unless there is firsthand experience with toxic behavior many are unaware of the tactics used by those who perpetrate abuse. In faith-based spaces, we operate under the ideal of loving our neighbors. It can be hard to fathom that a person could consciously choose to oppress those who reside in the same household with hard-hearted, calculated, malevolent acts. It is even harder to reconcile that fact if the abuser is a church member with a charismatic personality and display of good works throughout the congregation or community.

Churchgoing perpetrators seldom look like the characters in movies designed to make you feel uncomfortable. Often, they appear quite normal, and in some cases seem even better than average, especially in faith communities. It is very possible that people outside the home will not see the same version of the abusive spouse that the victim experiences behind closed doors. This is one way that abusers continue to get away with toxic behavior. Then, when those in the church choose to see only good in the perpetrator, victims are accused of overreacting or being untruthful.

Those outside the home may believe the perpetrator to be one of the best people they know—amiable, charming, humorous, kind, or even grandiose and generous—because that is the only version they have seen. But this carefully curated, false image is not what exists at home. The victim fell in love with and married the false image, but sometime after the wedding, the perpetrator removed the mask, and things began to change. One survivor described her abuser as engaging in equal-opportunity **misogyny**, starting right after the wedding. Over the years he claimed to hate his mother, his sister, his ex-wife, his daughter, and now he hated her as well.

When a victim brings a story of abuse to those who have never seen anything but the public (masked) version, it can be hard to reconcile the public image with what the victim is describing. This dissonance creates disbelief and causes people to discount what victims describe. Victims and survivors who take their faith literally are not making up wild tales. Statistics show that almost half of all abuse is unreported and that female victims are four times more likely than male victims to not report abuse due to fear of reprisal.[1]

We cannot simply assume that the one causing harm is like most people in our church. Most congregants possess an active conscience and would be grateful for constructive feedback about personal shortcomings. The perpetrator of abuse is not like this in that he or she often holds a sense of **entitlement**. These individuals feel the need to possess ultimate control over those who live in their homes. The entitled believe they have no need for correction, and they justify how they conduct themselves toward their families. This includes using Scripture to claim the authority to behave the way they do. Living a **double standard** is typical. While the abuser can do no wrong, the victim can't do anything right. Equality doesn't exist.

I know one story of an abusive spouse who said that "kindness was weakness." He thought that all pastors were unscrupulous individuals who took financial advantage of their congregations, and he would have had no trouble taking advantage of the pastor. Any attempt on the part of the church to help him would result in this abuser taking advantage of them in return. This was someone

---

1. Reaves, *Police Response to Domestic Violence*, 1.

who pretended to be a huge fan of the pastor while at church, but off church grounds would disparage the entire congregation to his wife and children.

An abuser may see a pastor's attempt at correction as a game, shedding a tear, expressing sorrow, and even asking for prayer. Feigned remorse and the pretense of working on the marriage will mislead faith leaders who are eager to see positive change. But it will not last, and most victims know this because they have seen patterns of insincere behavior, empty apologies, and broken promises. Victims have already forgiven the abusive spouse seventy times seven and provided numerous second chances. But lasting change never came.

A perpetrator will seldom offer a sincere apology with true regret, preferring instead to say the spouse started or caused the acts of poor behavior. One survivor related a time in which she asked for an apology, but all she received was a terse reply that he was sorry she was so stupid. An apology should never include excuses that minimize the abuse or deflect responsibility. Please be aware that you, as a faith leader, can be deceived and controlled just as the victim was. You may hear excuses and promises like the ones the victim has heard, but excuses and promises do not produce lasting change. Intention does not necessarily equal authentic action toward repentance. It simply allows the perpetrator prolonged control.

It is important to remember that abuse is a crime. Responding to or reporting abuse does less damage than not doing so. Holding someone accountable is part of justice (Prov 18:5). Allow professionals to handle any investigation or mediation. Cooperate with civil authorities. Support DV prevention, **battering intervention** programs, and protective orders. Be actively concerned for the protection of the victim and children. Be careful that you are not **colluding with the abuser**.

If you plan to engage in church discipline with the perpetrator, have a witness with you for accountability. Beware of risk to **bystanders**, including yourself and other congregants. If there is a known presence of weapons, understand that the risk increases.

Know that some church members may disagree or disapprove of your decision to engage in church discipline or remove a perpetrator from the congregation, declaring instead that the victim is the problem. However, Scripture warns against acquitting the guilty and condemning the innocent (Prov 17:15).

Genuine repentance takes time. Commitment to change deeply ingrained toxic attitudes and behaviors requires prolonged accountability. There must be strong boundaries, and each new standard for behavior must be adhered to with humility and meekness. The one who has perpetrated harm must recognize a personal pattern of ungodly behavior and take complete responsibility without blaming the victim.

Any change should include respect for the victim's autonomy and restitution for harm done. There must be no bullying, no threats to the victim or the church leadership, and no demanding of personal rights. The perpetrator should complete this work without the goal of reconciliation, couples counseling/family therapy, rescinding of restraining orders, or continued involvement at church. Doing it for those reasons is simply another means of manipulation. See appendix E for more about perpetrator accountability.

If there is ever to be reconciliation or any kind of joint couples therapy it must be on the victim's timetable, and only after much healing and professional, trauma-informed individual counseling for both parties. The accused should demonstrate fully changed behavior for at least a couple of years beyond any abusive relapse as the bare minimum. The reason for this prolonged timetable is that many perpetrators can imitate short-term compliance but cannot produce lasting change over time. Firm boundaries and the requirement of this commitment to change are necessary to keep the victim and children safe. Abusers who are unwilling to meet these requirements or put sustained effort into ongoing repentance are not safe and should not be in close proximity to those they have victimized.

I want to reiterate that DV is not a minor marital issue but rather a grievous choice to wield power and control over the spouse they vowed at the marriage altar to love and cherish for the rest of their lives. All forms of DV are directly opposite of God's love. Christ never abused the church, and abuse is never compatible with the Christian faith. The Scriptures clearly instruct us to put away violence and do what is right (Ezek 45:9). Abuse does not demonstrate love toward others (1 John 4:7–8, Gal 5:14). Verbal abuse is damaging (Prov 18:21, Matt 15:18, Eph 4:29, Jas 1:26). We are to avoid the deeds of the flesh (Gal 5:19–21). Proverbs 6 tells of the perverse, malicious, and contentious person and then outlines things that God hates: arrogance, lies, murder, wicked plans, mischief, a false witness, and a troublemaker who sows discord in the family.

As leaders in faith communities, we have an obligation to recognize DV and be part of the efforts to end it. These efforts include declaring all forms of abuse to be inconsistent with our faith, holding those who perpetrate abuse accountable for their actions, and offering the church's protection and resources to victims/survivors and their children. If you are working with the perpetrator, know that it is unwise for you to also work with the victim. One person cannot be fully dedicated to the needs of both individuals, and each party needs their own spiritual guidance without the risk of breaches in confidentiality. If necessary, you can partner with another faith leader so that each of you can provide care for the partners separately and safely, considering how to do that in a way that doesn't put either faith community at risk.

9

Consistent Conflict, It Really Is That Bad

EARLY IN AN ABUSIVE relationship, the conflict may be less constant. The perpetrator intersperses abuse with good times and positive memories to keep the victim off guard. This is purposeful. The intermittent reward-and-punishment cycle often creates **trauma bonds** between the abuser and the victim. Over time, victims learn to anticipate the violence and appease the toxic spouse to reduce conflict and keep some measure of peace in the home. But as a toxic relationship continues it is likely that the abuse becomes more frequent and more intense. The issue here is that the abuser controls everything, and thus holds all the power in the relationship. It is important to remember that the totality of abuse is likely much greater than what you see or hear from the victim.

Domestic violence is a circumstance in which abusers subject their spouses and children to ongoing, systemic violence within their own homes. Victims will attempt to find harmony, especially in homes where gentleness and peacekeeping are ideals they desire to live into. Victims who are earnest in their faith continue to return good for evil, hoping that their oppressors will eventually recognize their own harmful ways and display fully changed behavior.

Taking it Seriously

Abusers take advantage of this goodness and vulnerability by continuing to oppress those they know will respond with kindness.

Economic (or financial) abuse is one way that victims remain dependent on their spouses. If women are not employed, or do not have free and equal access to financial accounts, that dependency increases, and self-sufficiency decreases even further. Economic dependence combined with traditional gender roles increases the risk and severity of DV.[1] Ideology about men as heads of the household, especially in financial matters, has given women less financial stability and granted immunity to those who perpetrate financial harm toward their families. Not everyone knows about the connection of economic abuse to DV; however, almost all survivors have experienced it.[2] The combination of abuse, economic control, and thoughts of pending poverty after separation or divorce due to lack of finances may keep victims in the relationship longer than is safe.

Female victims of abuse have shared that their husbands had bank accounts that they had no access to and that their husbands gave them a minuscule allowance to purchase food and household items. One victim reported spending less than two dollars over the allotted food budget and her husband required that she return the offending product back to the store for a refund. Another husband limited his victim to 150 dollars a week for grocery money after she fled intense abuse, despite his earning a six-figure income.

Some abusers do not allow their spouses to have a job. In other cases, the abuser may stay home and do nothing while requiring that the spouse work. Abusers have tied their victims to beds and locked them out of their own homes. Men with destructive spouses have been on the receiving end of thrown scissors, flying glassware, broken wine bottles, lies about their careers, verbal vitriol, spouses who wouldn't come home, drug and alcohol misuse, and neglect.

Survivors interviewed for the CC&DV research spoke of their **isolation** as their abuser moved them from state to state, across

1. Moulding et al., "Rethinking Women's Mental Health," 1065.
2. Postmus et al., "Understanding Economic Abuse," 411–12.

the country, or even out of the country. This isolation meant they no longer had access to family, friends, and other individuals and groups who could have provided them with support. Manipulation and criticism were frequent. There was belittling about the food they cooked, the clothing they wore, or how much they weighed. There were threats to wreck the car if the children cried during trips or outings. There were threats that they would never see their children again if they didn't comply with random requests. One abuser had his mistress living in the same household.

Gaslighting, a form of psychological abuse, was common. One husband sought to drive his wife crazy by secretly moving and taking objects from her dressing table for months. He had been telling her that she just never remembered where she put things and that she was losing her mind until she began to believe it. This is also known as **crazy making**, and you can probably see why that term exists. The survivors described perpetrators with a need for constant control. Some survivors shared that while still in their abusive marriages, they did not have the freedom to do simple things like read books, wear makeup, visit family, have a private phone or text conversation, buy name-brand products, or use the family vehicle. One survivor mentioned not being allowed to sleep in a bed if she didn't behave in his desired way.

Missing belongings. Incessant screaming. Missing pets. Destruction of property. Refusal to work. Drug use. Reckless driving. Dragged by the hair down the hall. Infidelity. Punched in the face. Denied medical attention. Living in squalor. Repeated **strangulation** to the point of passing out. Frequent rape and sexual assault. Staring down the barrel of a loaded gun. Shot from close range. These are just some of the horrible experiences that I have personally heard about from survivors of DV. In many cases, these were not one-time happenings but repeated practices. It is that bad, and sometimes it's worse. At the heart of coercive control is a lack of liberty, lack of choice, and lack of autonomy for the victim.[3] These victims have described feeling like prisoners in their own homes.

---

3. Moulding et al., "Rethinking Women's Mental Health," 1072.

Such are situations in which victims of abuse have heard from their faith leaders that they may not leave and certainly cannot file for divorce. They heard that prayer and submission would end the abuse, or even that the abuse was God's will. One victim shared hearing that if her husband had killed her that at least she would have died for a righteous cause. Some victims attended multiple churches during the marriage, none of them with a good understanding of abuse. Some pastors asked these victims what they did to cause the abuse. Others disallowed victims to seek counseling outside the church. In other cases, the church dismissed the truth, or disfellowshipped victims for seeking safety.

I share these tragic circumstances not to vilify the church but to speak plainly about real-life experiences shared in personal conversations and interviews. It can be easy to be deceived by what may appear to be the calm, collected, at-ease manner of the abusive spouse. It then becomes easier to villainize the victim who may appear withdrawn, confused, elusive, and depressed. When victims do present poorly the toxic spouse may use that to further disparage your views of the victim by claiming the victim has mental health issues and ungodly attitudes. It can be easier to blame the timid, frazzled spouse than the more powerful one because of the effort required to address toxic attitudes and behaviors.

Survivors I have spoken with have lamented over the Christian marriage books they read, books that asserted that wives could fix the behavior of their husbands through their own actions. If the husband was disagreeable, it was up to her to fix things not just with prayer but also with better meals, a cleaner home, further submission, and more sex. However, in an abusive relationship, sex is weaponized. Sheila Wray Gregoire has become well known through her research on sexuality within the Christian tradition. In her book *Rescuing and Reframing Common Evangelical Teachings about Sex and Marriage*, she states that reducing sex to something women do to meet men's needs creates entitlement for men and obligation for women. Obligation reduces mutual satisfaction in intimacy, and entitlement leads to the dismissal of marital rape.[4]

---

4. Gregoire, *Rescuing and Reframing*, loc. 117.

When marital rape is dismissed, these victims must continue to live with their rapists, cooking their meals, washing their clothes, and cleaning their houses. They do this, knowing that assault could happen again at any time. Female survivors have shared about succumbing to sexual assault and rape to distract their husbands or try to calm them down. Some abusers have told their spouses that if they don't provide sex, it will turn them to pornography or affairs, and then they do that anyway. They may require that their spouses mimic what they have viewed in their rampant porn addiction. They may require sexual favors for grocery money or the privilege to go to church. Other abusers withhold sex and affection as a form of punishment. None of this solves the issues in an abusive marriage. No effort on the part of the victim will heal an abusive spouse. The consistent conflict carries on.

10

Spiritual Weariness Runs Deep

ABUSE CREATES NOT JUST a moment of frustration but rather a profound ache deep in the soul. The longer someone has been in an abusive marriage, the deeper that weariness goes. As humans, we all experience some level of distress as part of life, but the anguish that one endures due to DV permeates the body, spirit, and soul. Victims share their vulnerabilities with their spouses because they honestly believe this is what marriage is about, and in a healthy relationship, it should be. But in a toxic relationship, vulnerability can lead to neglect, abuse, and harm. What is shared in confidence becomes fuel for perpetrators to use against them as part of the abuse. Betrayal by a spouse who has vowed love, honor, and protection is brutal. It is a Judas kiss.

In the CC&DV research, I received mixed responses to a question for survivors about their view of God during the abuse. One survivor spoke of seeing God as a shield from the beatings, another said God was a rescuer, and others felt the presence of God more strongly. However, some survivors talked of how they could not feel God's presence. One cried out to God, struggling to figure out what God wanted of her. One mentioned how growing up in a legalistic church made her feel like she was never good enough. Another talked of Christianity as a form of oppression. A couple of survivors were mad at God and mad at the church. One asked God for discernment in his life only to have his marriage fall apart. These wounds are deep and painful.

Abuse attacks not only who someone is as an individual. In a so-called Christian home, it attacks who that person is in Christ. Female survivors whom I have spoken with have heard from their spouses that God does not love them because they are only women, that God expects submission in all things, and that women must be subservient. In addition to such statements, the abusers attacked their faith, spiritual practices, and desire to attend church. They married believing faith was common ground but soon discovered that their spouses had little to no interest in faith at all.

I am familiar with one situation in which a woman was beaten many times. She reached out to her husband's family (his father was a preacher) for help, but they told her it was her fault and that she should have been a better wife. Such a response could have had fatal consequences, but thankfully, she got out and sought a divorce, which probably saved her life. She continued to attend church, but as a divorcee, she lived in fear for her soul due to the church's teachings on divorce. As an elderly woman, she was fearful of death because she didn't know if God would admit her into heaven. I have heard other stories in which a woman's abusive spouse was a leader in their church, publicly claiming God's authority and yet harming his family at home.

Female victims and survivors report having attended churches that teach a version of God that demands that they be second-class servants in their marriages. I have seen this not just in my own research but in mainstream conversations as well. A recent news story revealed how one church has a history of mishandling domestic violence, requiring that women submit and reconcile with abusive husbands, and even providing written support for the men.[1] Another news story mentioned a church where women cannot say no, and men were to conquer and colonize their wives.[2] Surely, this is neither God's design for marriage nor for the church.

---

1. Shellnutt, "Grace Community Church Rejected."
2. Stankorb, "Inside the Church."

Taking it Seriously

Harsh treatment and reprimands by faith communities who claim this is the way of the Lord make God seem as cruel and unloving as the abuser. Survivors I have spoken with would like their pastors and churches to stop using insensitive comments and to recognize that verbal and emotional abuse is very damaging. They want to be believed when they speak up about the agonizing issues affecting them and their children. They want their faith communities to pay attention, define abuse broadly, and understand that DV is not something easily fixed.

Religion can be both a risk, due to the acceptance of force and control in marriage, and a protective factor, in offering comfort and hope.[3] An abusive spouse's attack on the victim's faith can lead to questioning and confusion. Victims may struggle with their faith, while simultaneously clinging to God for the strength to endure each day. Their faith is a lifeline in the storm that helps them survive the horrors of years or even decades of abuse, but they are unsure about God's love when they hear theology that condemns them to stay in abuse without protection.

Victims and survivors of DV may need to know why God allowed the abuse to happen, or why God did not intervene and deliver them in their time of need. They may wonder if their faith was not strong enough. They especially need the care of a faith community but may be hesitant to seek help due to weariness or the perceived social stigma around the issues of abuse and divorce. They will need your attention to these matters. Whether you serve in a paid ministerial position or as a lay leader in a church or faith-based organization, it is vital that you know how to respond well to victims and survivors of DV. Pastoral care in its most general sense is practiced by all those who minister to others in a faith-based environment, including the provision of emotional, social, and spiritual support.

In my work with victims and survivors of DV, I have learned that it is not their faith that has produced a real struggle for them, but the church. It grieves me that the institution representing God has produced harm. There is no room for judgment against

---

3. McMullin et al., "When Violence Hits," 114.

those who have experienced abuse, and we need to guard against complacency regarding those perpetrating DV. We can work to actively create safe spaces as we share God's love and serve with open hearts and hands. Good works are the action of our faith (Jas 2:14) and lend authenticity to our message.

Survivors who struggled with how their church responded often still found an individual or two who were helpful and understanding of their circumstances, though sometimes that support came from outside the church. While even just one supportive person can make a difference, the purpose of this book is to increase the support that survivors find within the church. The lasting impact of full support truly makes a significant contribution to the lives of survivors and their children.

One survivor stated that victims of abuse can find more welcome, compassion, and understanding outside the church than in it. When victims and survivors believe that their help will come from secular sources before it comes from the church, we have evidence that we need to increase safety and support for them within our sacred spaces. We can help them tap into a faith in which they keenly feel God's love and care. We can listen for cries of distress. We can offer resources in times of need. We can work to restore the soul and spirit of the wounded. Jesus insisted that those who are weary with heavy burdens could come to him for rest (Matt 11:28). The tired and wounded should feel they can fully rest in the healing arms of God. We must be proactive in making sure our faith communities reflect that.

We must be careful that our faith communities do not malign women. The Bible is quite progressive about featuring women and liberating them. In the Old Testament, Hagar (Gen 16:1–13) was a slave treated harshly by her mistress. In her distress, she fled, but God met her where she was. God called her by name, and Hagar became the first person—a woman, a foreigner, and a slave—to name God. She called God *El Roi*, the God who sees. In the New Testament, it was Mary Magdalene (John 20:11–18) whom Jesus sent to tell the disciples the good news of his resurrection. These are just two of many examples of God giving prominence to women. For those who have experienced DV, it helps to see that God uses and features women in the work of the kingdom. This offers encouragement in the long journey toward healing.

As we consider how abuse and coercive control violate the Bible's instructions for godly living, we can draw from much of Scripture. Just a few examples follow: What comes out of a person from the inside defiles them (Mark 7:20–23). The acts of the flesh demonstrate immorality, hatred, discord, jealousy, and rage (Gal 5:19–21). Considering oneself to be religious, but not controlling the tongue, renders that religion worthless (Jas 1:26). There are instructions to not speak falsely, to speak only wholesome language, to get rid of anger and malice, and to be kind and compassionate (Eph 4:25–32). Those who do not provide for their households have denied the faith (1 Tim 5:8). Those who do not love others do not know God (1 John 4:8).

Yet survivors know that throwing a few Bible verses at the abuser while asking for an apology is not going to fix it. To overturn the attitudes and behaviors that perpetrators use against their victims requires years of intentional work with highly trained practitioners. Faith leaders should recognize the incredible harm that consistent conflict does to the victims in these marriages as the physical, emotional, and spiritual weariness sets in. The church's lack of understanding or compassion toward the victim only furthers the agony experienced and damages the reputation of our faith, possibly driving victims and survivors of DV away from the church forever. We must take this seriously.

11

Why Victims Might Stay in the Abuse

SOME QUESTION WHY, IF it's really that bad, a victim of DV stays in the relationship. This chapter will outline many reasons, but asking why people stay in the abuse shifts the question in the wrong direction. As many advocates have brought to light, we should be asking what keeps them there. What keeps them so ensnared that they cannot easily get out? What has society, and more importantly what has the church, done to keep victims trapped in these destructive relationships? We should also ask why perpetrators are abusing their victims in the first place and seek information about how that is being addressed.

In examining these questions, we can consider the safety and survival of those experiencing abuse. The social media **hashtags** in the glossary highlight the plight of some specific victims, but in this chapter, you will see that there are many reasons that victims stay, many of them rooted in fear. Women of faith tend to stay longer in abusive relationships and have greater barriers to changing their circumstances, in some cases feeling they must choose between their faith and their freedom.[1]

---

1. Drumm et al., "God Just Brought Me," 386.

Some victims stay because they do not know what a healthy relationship looks like or how to recognize abusive behavior. If they grew up in a home where DV was present, the abuse feels normal. In these cases, it is possible that they married to escape the abuse at home only to end up in an abusive marriage. They often cling to the hope that things will change. They believe that love will conquer all, and they pour 110 percent of their energy into that. Most victims truly want their marriage to succeed and go to great lengths to nurture it. They believe that trying harder will help. They consistently devote themselves to the relationship and are not quick to give up.

All forms of DV can render a victim powerless to make a change. Perpetrators will isolate the victim from any form of support: family, friends, church, work colleagues, community resources, and more. Frequent moves are not uncommon. Moving to a new place without support is challenging. The emotional turmoil from years of abuse leaves them with doubts and uncertainties that make it hard to make decisions. Fear and low self-esteem can factor into feelings of powerlessness. Psychological and verbal assaults can leave a victim just as afraid and entangled as situations of physical and sexual abuse. Occasional assault interspersed with threats of harm is usually enough to keep the victim in line.

Whether it is ongoing or intermittent, violence reinforces unhealthy and unequal power dynamics in the relationship. Without knowledge of the cycle of abuse with its occasional reprieves from toxic behavior, victims may think during the calmer times that an incident of abuse was a mistake or just a bad day and continue to offer numerous second chances to an oppressive spouse who has no intention of changing. Victims may think they deserve the treatment they receive. They stay because the abuser has manipulated and brainwashed them. They have been told they are responsible for the abusive behavior, and they don't know differently.

The perpetrator's influence in the community can be a reason the victim stays, particularly if he has a powerful or high-profile career. When the abusive spouse is a politician, judge, police officer, physician, athletic coach, nonprofit director, attorney, bank president, university professor, or pastor the victim fears not only personal retribution but also public scrutiny and contempt from those who know nothing about the situation. One survivor explained how military officials really didn't seem to care that her husband had abused her. Another, whose husband was a first responder, struggled to get justice in the courts. Toxic individuals will often seek positions of power and use that to their advantage, which puts their victims at a decided disadvantage.

Victims often stay in DV situations due to a lack of finances. Women in their midlife years who have stayed home to raise children say it is difficult to leave because starting over without education and work experience makes earning a living wage quite difficult. Without an adequate job, a good credit history, or cash reserves, it can be quite difficult to secure a safe place to live after leaving the abuse. Some victims don't even have their names on the vehicle titles, making transportation inaccessible. If they need an attorney, securing one without a sizable retainer is nearly impossible. Feeding and clothing children and paying for utilities and insurance can be outside the financial reach of single parents. The prospect of struggling to make ends meet once away from the abuse can be overwhelming.

Victims will stay in the abuse out of fear of what may happen to their children. Numerous survivors have told me that they stayed to protect children from potentially dangerous situations. These women would put themselves in harm's way to be an obstacle when a spouse was angry. Victims have heard from their churches that divorce is bad for children, but not that divorce is better for them than a toxic home. They have not heard the truth about the negative effects that long-term abuse has on children.[2] They are afraid of what could happen to the children on unsupervised visits after a divorce. Family court can be daunting and exceedingly expensive. In some cases, victims think it is easier to stay and handle what is known rather than deal with the unknown. The ultimate fear for a victim of abuse is to lose the children to the very person who may hurt them. Courts have granted custody even to fathers

2. Baskerville, "Is It Always Best."

who physically abuse and sexually molest their children because the officials do not believe mothers about these dreadful crimes, demonstrating a continued bias against women in the courts.[3]

Some stay in the abuse due to personal struggles with mental health concerns and a fear of being further villainized by the abusive spouse. Those who take anxiety or depression medication because of the abuse they have experienced have found that court proceedings and custody battles are against them. Judges and court personnel generally do not have enough training on DV to quickly sort out which parent is the safer choice, and in these cases, they may give custody to the abusive parent due to mental health allegations against the victim.

Cultural differences may keep someone in the abuse. These can be ethnic, familial, social, or religious. Some individuals stay in the abuse because that is what their family of origin told them is the right thing to do, or because their church expected it. Local authorities do not always see victims as sincere. Dual arrest policies have led to an increase in Black women being arrested when they call authorities about abuse.[4] Those in the LGBTQ+ community may continue to stay in abusive relationships because they already feel judgment from the church regarding their identity. Male victims of abuse may stay because they find that no one believes that their physically smaller spouses abuse them. Elderly and disabled victims may stay because of physical and financial dependency on their spouses.

Pets are another reason that victims choose to stay in situations of DV. Victims of abuse will stay in, or return to, toxic situations rather than leave pets behind, and many report that their abuser threatened to kill or injure a pet.[5] A new housing situation may not allow pets, or a lack of finances may limit the ability to provide adequate care for their animals. Many DV shelters do not have adequate kennel space for their clients to bring pets when they stay in the shelter. Pet abuse is common in cases of DV, and

3. Meier and Dickson, "Mapping Gender," 312–13.
4. Shinde, "Black Women, Police Brutality," 2.
5. Philips, "Understanding the Link," 9.

many victims and their children cannot bear to leave beloved pets behind.

Not knowing the definition of DV and what it may look like in everyday life keeps many victims in the abuse. Thinking that DV only consists of physical assault is a common misconception that ignores all the other forms of destruction that happen in abusive relationships. When society minimizes the abuse or engages in **blame shifting**, the situation becomes very confusing. Victims may doubt what they experienced when the perpetrator makes excuses or lies about the details of a situation. Victims also tend to engage in self-blame until they themselves fully understand the truth of DV. Denial of how bad things have gotten is common. It is like the proverbial frog that doesn't realize it is being boiled alive because the temperature of the water rises slowly. As the abuse grows steadily worse, the behavior becomes normalized in the relationship.

Some will stay in a toxic or abusive marriage because they have received counsel that faithful prayers will cure the relationship. Believing this to be so, they literally pray continually (1 Thess 5:17) or pray the prayer of the afflicted (Jas 5:15). They trust that prayers of faith will save their marriage, and yet the abuse continues. I know of devoted women who donned head coverings while in prayer, wondering if that would make a difference in their petitions, only to be ridiculed by their abusers. The women whom I have spoken with about prayer for their marriages and spouses are like the persistent widow in Luke 18, pleading for justice against the adversary, continuing to lament over unanswered prayers.

Some will stay in dangerous DV situations because they have never heard from their church that God hates abuse. Instead, they may have heard from the pulpit that God hates divorce, that marriage is forever, and that this is their cross to bear in life. They may believe it is their sole responsibility to fix the marriage or hold things together. But they have never heard anyone speak about how abuse destroys marriages and harms the individuals in the home. They have never heard that God hates evil and cares for the oppressed, having heard only versions of **doormat theology** that required more submission, more forgiveness, and more prayer.

These are just some of the reasons a victim will stay in the abuse. Keep in mind that each situation is unique. A pastor or faith leader can help mitigate some of these reasons, while others may take a coordinated effort. Start with increasing DV awareness. Refer those experiencing abuse to the appropriate community resources, provide support networks, assist with finances, and help with children and pets. Be aware of and sensitive to cultural differences and mental health. Ask what is needed most.

This is your opportunity to show the protection of God for the oppressed and display the love of God that heals wounds. Where members of the clergy, chaplains, and faith-based counselors will be especially helpful to those struggling with DV is what pertains to faith: hope, doubt, shame, fear, scriptural interpretation, and views of God. If you take abuse seriously, victims will too.

12

Domestic Violence and Marriage

MARRIAGE HAS BEEN A sacred institution within the church for millennia, and faith leaders may be hesitant to blame marriage for the abuse and harm that victims experience. Christian culture often reveres the nuclear family.[1] Strongly worded ideals about marriage and expected gender roles may prioritize the value of men as leaders over the exposure of women to any of the many forms of abuse.

Interviews from my research revealed that this often came down to men demanding submission. Survivors mentioned needing to be subordinate to the husband and that there were expectations for how to fulfill wifely duties correctly. One had to quit her job, another was not allowed to have flowers in her yard, and another had to ask permission to go to the store. Keep in mind that these men were demanding submission from women of faith who already desired to keep their marriages together. These women were already submitting, and it was costing them dearly.

To successfully address DV we must talk about marriage. Most abuse will happen at home, behind closed doors. In this way, one spouse can dominate the other without witnesses. Telling female victims that they need to be more obedient or male victims

---

1. Collins, *Out of Control*, loc. 55.

that they need to selflessly love the one who is destroying them will not end the abuse. Perceived **guilt**, shame, and embarrassment keep the abused partner silent. Confusion and questions surface: How did this happen? Why is the person they love hurting them? And what will make the abuse stop?

Female survivors of DV interviewed for the CC&DV research said their church would tell them that the job of keeping the marriage intact was their responsibility because they are the helpmeet, never once hearing condemnation for abuse. Women reported hearing that the abuse would end if they would just be better wives. Church leaders told them to be less willful, less talkative, less harsh, and less controlling. Sermons and other messages heard at church instructed them to be kinder, gentler, more understanding, more giving, more forgiving, and certainly more submissive. They did work on their marriages, and the abuse continued to get worse. We cannot expect a victim to hold together what the perpetrator is unwilling to work on.

Gender role expectations and hierarchical structures in some families and faith communities heap guilt and obligation upon women to keep the relationship intact, while limiting options for agency and escape.[2] If the couple belongs to a faith community with rigid power structures and strict gender roles, there is relief neither at home nor at church. My interviews with survivors included conversations about sermons that instructed women concerning their duties in the home but no such messages to husbands about servant leadership and kindness. Even a male victim of abuse mentioned that this was the case, acknowledging gender bias in the church.

Survivors of abuse described how church leaders told them that the abuse they endured was for their sanctification and that marriage was meant to make them holy. Women in abusive marriages have been instructed to embrace hardship the way Jesus did on the cross. They were told to endure abuse patiently. They have literally heard that their suffering glorifies God. But the suffering of Jesus and the abuse that victims experience are not the same,

---

2. Nash, "Changing of the Gods," 195–96.

and it is illogical to equate the two. In the words of Steven Tracy, Jesus suffered *for* our sins; victims of DV suffer *because of* sin (emphasis mine).³ He goes on to remind us that the redemptive quality of Jesus' suffering is due to the fact that he is God, not that he suffered in silence.⁴ Let's make sure we do not compare enduring abuse with the sacrifice Jesus made for the sins of the world, or say that God asks victims to suffer in this way. God is not an author of confusion.

In preparing for my research, I found that encouraging victims to suffer as Jesus did was not an anomaly. Multiple DV studies reported a belief by both clergy and victims that suffering was virtuous or a sign of honor.⁵ Religious language ties submission to male leadership, and if a woman is subject to abuse and suffering at home, that is simply her lot in life.⁶ And yet submission and prayer have not proven to be effective in the prevention of DV.⁷ The interviews with survivors echoed this. If we want to ask victims of abuse to mimic Jesus, there are other examples we can use. More than once, Jesus walked away from those who sought to kill him (Matt 12:14–15, Luke 4:28–30, John 8:58–59).

Victims and survivors of abuse and assault often feel they have little ability to change their situations. Then, in that vulnerable state, they experience little empathy from their faith leaders or churches. They have described being ignored, disparaged, and further oppressed. To **marginalize** DV victims is to view their experiences as unimportant. It happens when church authorities silence them, minimize the abuse, support their abuser, and ostracize them because they don't return to dangerous homes. When an institution establishes men as the final authority and does not

---

3. Tracy, "Domestic Violence in the Church," 292.

4. Tracy, "Domestic Violence in the Church," 293.

5. Shannon-Lewy and Dull, "Response of Christian Clergy," 651; Rotunda et al., "Clergy Response," 355; Nason-Clark et al., *Religion and Intimate Partner Violence*, 1.

6. Westenberg, "When She Calls for Help," 2.

7. Nash, "Changing of the Gods," 205.

grant protection to women, it allows subjection to continue with what appears to be the blessing of the church.

Within faith communities, few, if any, female victims are provoking their husbands to wrath. Instead, they are doing all they can to improve the marriage because they want the abuse to end. They have read books that required obedience to husbands above all else, even if told to sin.[8] Such a thought process leaves victims confused. These victims absolutely felt it was wrong to sin yet wondered about perplexing instructions that they were to comply with their husbands' requests for wrongdoing, particularly in areas of sexual sin. Such teaching is at odds with the verse that instructs us to obey God rather than man (Acts 5:29).

The survivors interviewed for the CC&DV research mentioned that churches were not aware of the signs of abuse and that pastors were unprepared to help. One seminary-trained survivor agreed that his experience supported this. Unhelpful comments included pushing through the pain, praying that things would improve, blocking memories of the abuse, or stating that husbands just needed more sex or that it was a mutual sin issue. One survivor stated that some churches don't recognize abuse or **rape in marriage**. Others didn't feel their church was a safe place to share the truth about what they lived with. One, however, did state that if the pastor had known maybe he would have asked if she were okay, and another survivor acknowledged receiving an apology from a pastor years later.

Churches have disciplined victims for leaving abusive marriages and not reconciling with their abusers. I conversed with a survivor whose pastor would not speak to her and dismissed her from the church because her abusive husband claimed that she left the marriage due to his pornography problem. Leaving due to the porn problem should have been sufficient, but the truth was that she left due to multiple incidents of strangulation causing her to lose consciousness in addition to other serious acts of harm. Strangulation is a serious marker of **lethality**.

---

8. Tracy, "Clergy Responses to Domestic Violence," 9.

DOMESTIC VIOLENCE AND MARRIAGE

It would be presumptuous to tell a victim of abuse that God will provide protection in marriage. That may be true, but it is also true that sometimes evil continues unchecked. For the victims to whom God did not grant protection, how will they feel when given such a statement? Will they feel unworthy of protection and unloved by God? How will you, as a leader in a faith-based institution, explain the lack of protection? A lack of protection does not equal sinfulness, unworthiness, or judgment from God. Consider the story of Job, the most righteous man who walked the earth. He endured intense affliction, and lost everything. There are long-held beliefs that illness and calamity are due to sin, but Job's story shows that tragedy can happen even to the most devoted.

Why do many women, especially those immersed in purity culture, end up victimized by the men they believed were the answer to their honest prayers for a godly spouse? Survivors of abuse have expressed to me that they wished they had not bought into the purity culture movement. Parents of DV victims and clergy sexual assault survivors have said the same. The strict gender roles, modesty, and pledges of abstinence within purity culture ideology were often one-sided, placing blame and shame on females, without holding males to the same strict standards of conduct.

Some individuals believed they could have left an unhealthy relationship if it were not for the church's beliefs about premarital sex that trapped them—sex a boy they met at church coerced them into having—only to have their churches add to the guilt and pronounce them damaged. Such rhetoric can force women into marrying someone who is already abusing them, particularly if pregnancy is involved, rather than offering a safe path out of a toxic relationship. Conversations about consent and dating violence are vital, even (or especially) at church.

Sexual coercion is rape. Pressuring someone into sex, and ignoring dissent, is coercion and rape. There must be full, ongoing, enthusiastic consent—even in marriage. When a spouse does not have autonomy and gives in to sexual pressure because she knows not doing so will result in another form of abuse, this is assault and rape. A helpful description for authentic consent is the ability to say *no* and have that *no* be respected.⁹ We should acknowledge that individuals have the freedom to change their minds. Intimacy should never be forced or expected as a marital duty, and no spouse should ever be degraded in the bedroom as often happens when abusive partners have sexual addictions or use porn. Pornography conditions men to violate their spouses.¹⁰ These marriages don't improve. They get worse.

Marriage should not be a war in which one spouse actively seeks to destroy the other. Marriage should feel safe. It should *be* safe. Verbal and emotional harassment has no place in marriage. Neither spouse should ever have to fear the other. Marriage should promote open communication, where both spouses can freely share without getting into trouble. Both spouses should radiate the fruit of the Spirit: love, joy, peace, forbearance, kindness, goodness, faithfulness, and self-control (Gal 5:22–23). Each spouse's character should reflect integrity, especially behind closed doors when no one is watching.

We cannot treat problems in unhealthy relationships the same as issues in marriages that are basically healthy. The dynamics are drastically different. Toxic relationships do not resolve conflict through the fair exchange of conversation and reflection, but rather stoop to unjust tactics that include verbal, emotional, or physical abuse. Treating abuse should not be focused on grace and **forgiveness**. I realize that may sound blunt, but victims have already granted that. They have given in to petty and manipulative behaviors to keep the peace. They have minimized themselves to the point of barely existing. Victims and survivors need churches to start responding with justice.

Conversations and actions regarding toxic marriages need to be about holding perpetrators of harm accountable. Then, if the perpetrator demonstrates repentance and changed behavior over time, grace and forgiveness can enter the discussion. We can honor the sanctity of marriage and protect victims of abuse. They are not mutually exclusive. In fact, we honor the sanctity of

---

9. Fortune, *Love Does No Harm*, 27.
10. Nason-Clark et al., *Religion and Intimate Partner Violence*, 8.

marriage through our expectation of godly attitudes and behavior. We honor marriage when it reflects integrity and respect from both partners equally.

Even if you and your church do not support the harmful ideas and practices mentioned in this chapter, those who have experienced harm elsewhere may end up in your congregation. Victims and survivors may visit your church after another faith community has asked them to leave, or after experiencing a lack of compassion about their circumstances. Knowing how victims have been oppressed in marriage and faith-based settings is essential to your ability to help these individuals. As leaders in faith-based settings, we all have an opportunity to love and support those who struggle under the weight of oppression. May God's divine mercy shine through us as we do, and may that grant hope to the survivors we encounter.

13

Domestic Violence and Divorce

ABUSE DESTROYS THE COVENANT of marriage by breaking the promise to love, honor, and cherish the spouse. The willful choice to engage in an ongoing pattern of destructive behavior displays continuous abandonment of the other spouse emotionally, physically, and spiritually. Additionally, pornography and sexual addictions comprise infidelities that release victims from destructive marriages. The Scriptures tell us that the eye is the lamp of the body, and if the eyes are bad, the whole body is dark (Matt 6:23).

There are already authors with multiple works online and in print that detail divorce and the Bible in great depth. See appendix A for resources about that. This book focuses more on pastoral care and congregational preparedness. Victims of abuse are not looking for an easy way out of their marriage. They generally want their marriages to work, and they have dedicated themselves to that for years or even decades. They have invested deeply in their relationship, and the depth of that investment can make it hard to acknowledge the DV or the need to seek safety.

However, when an abusive spouse literally destroys every effort, when the verbal and psychological aggression won't cease, when there is ongoing neglect, when there is excessive alcohol or drug use, when there is porn addiction, when there is property damage, if there is harm to the children, or when the death threats won't end, there must be an option to protect the victim and children. To those who may be uneasy about allowing divorce for abuse, I hear you. Church teaching, both past and present, has largely been against divorce. Many victims have heard from their faith communities that abuse is not a justification for separation or divorce.

Can we agree that God established marriage for humans and not the other way around? God does not enslave humans to the institution of marriage, nor should the church sacrifice victims on the altar of marriage. That is the language that many Christian DV advocates use in describing the inflexibility of faith leaders on this issue. They have noticed that the institution of marriage is an altar on which some churches sacrifice victims of abuse. The many advocates who use this language have a point. Requiring victims to stay in the abuse due to the ideal of marriage permanence puts the institution of marriage above the safety of the individual. Quite frankly, it sets up marriage as an idol.

We cannot ignore or further injure those who are being abused. We cannot sacrifice children on the altar of marriage either. Requiring that a marriage stay together for the sake of the kids doesn't make sense. Witnessing and experiencing abuse has life-altering effects on children and predisposes them to perpetrate abuse or be further victimized later in life.[1] Studies have shown that children fare better with divorce than with staying in an abusive home.[2] Divorce after abuse does not weaken the family but rather strengthens those affected to break the cycle of violence. This protects future generations from experiencing the same fate.

A third of the survivors in the CC&DV qualitative interviews mentioned that the church was more concerned about a pending divorce than the abuse that they were experiencing. Only one survivor mentioned that her church was okay with the divorce due to abusive behavior. The first time she sought help, however, the church encouraged her to reconcile. Another survivor mentioned that sermons need to stop mentioning children from **broken**

1. CDC, "About Child Abuse and Neglect."
2. Baskerville, "Is It Always Best."

homes when speaking about divorce, which is a good suggestion. We must keep in mind that it is abuse that breaks the home and causes the demise of the marriage. Church focus should be on the use of ungodly behavior, not the divorce itself. Some survivors had pastors tell them that they could not speak of the abuse to others outside the home because that would equal the sin of gossip, but telling the truth and seeking assistance is not gossip. The Scriptures clearly insist that we do speak the truth (Eph 4:25), expose darkness (Eph 5:11), and reject every form of evil (1 Thess 5:22). These survivors followed Scripture in speaking up about abuse.

I understand that this book discusses a lot of negative content, so let me tell you a positive. I had a pastor inform me the other day that while preaching through Proverbs he began including qualifiers and caveats when talking about conflict, relationships, and abuse with the tongue. In a sermon about gossip and speaking ill of others, he included information on what that doesn't mean. It doesn't mean that you don't report harmful, illegal, or abusive behaviors. He understood how some might twist Scripture with evil intent and took care to make sure his congregation was appropriately informed. I loved that and thanked him for his attention to detail.

My survivor interviews described situations where the pastors were against divorce or required submission and staying in the abuse. However, the results of the faith leader survey regarding divorce were interesting. Sixty-five percent responded that they were not against divorce in cases of any kind of abuse, 21 percent were unsure about how they would counsel congregants about divorce, 6 percent said only after attempted reconciliation, 4 percent said they would allow it in cases of physical abuse, and 3 percent would either never recommend divorce or be okay with it only if there was also adultery or abandonment.

The differences between the survivor interviews and the faith leaders surveyed could be due to varying faith traditions, denominational teachings about divorce, pastoral awareness, level of education, or even geographic location, but the gap between them was certainly intriguing. My survey results revealed that 63 percent of faith leaders believed that *divorce* breaks the covenant of marriage, with male faith leaders being more likely to agree than female faith leaders.[3] However, 96 percent of all respondents believed that *abuse* breaks the covenant of marriage.

For those who have experienced DV, that is an encouraging response. Regarding a question about divorce being the best way to protect a victim of abuse, the faith leaders split, with 52 percent agreeing and 48 percent disagreeing. When assessed for differences, females were more in agreement with this statement than males, pastors more than non-pastors, those with graduate degrees more than those without graduate degrees, and those aged fifty-nine and under were more in agreement than those aged sixty and older, but none of these differences was statistically significant.[4]

It is important that you know that separation or divorce is generally not the end of the matter. In his book *The Quincy Solution*, Barry Goldstein writes of seeing many cases where a father who wanted little to do with his children during the marriage suddenly and aggressively sought custody of the children, knowing it was a sure way to devastate a former spouse.[5] Sadly, some are motivated by revenge to use the courts to punish their victims, even to the point of taking the children away from the parent who is desperately trying to protect them.

Such behavior is not unusual in cases of DV. Many abusive individuals will continue their toxic behavior even if the marriage ends, and some will find new ways to punish a spouse for seeking safety. To manage ongoing difficulties after separation, survivors will use strategies like **gray rock** or **yellow rock** to minimize conflict and establish boundaries. In some cases, courts will issue **no contact** orders between the two parties. If a divorce occurs, know that custody laws and family courts vary from state to state and that the process is lengthy, emotionally exhausting, and expensive. Survivors of abuse will need your support to make it through these situations. Accompany the survivor to court appearances to be

---

3. Goertzen and Fox, "Response of Christian Faith."
4. Goertzen and Fox, "Response of Christian Faith."
5. Goldstein, *Quincy Solution*, loc. 1535–39.

there as a visible support person for the one who has been harmed by abuse.

Post-separation abuse can be particularly dangerous. Barry Goldstein warns us that 75 percent of women murdered by their partners are killed around the time they try to leave, or soon after leaving the relationship.[6] It is as if the abuser is seeking a final and fatal form of power and control over the victim. Prior incidence of strangulation raises the risk of death 750 percent.[7] The presence of weapons significantly raises the risk.[8] Guns raise the risk of domestic homicide by over 500 percent.[9] Women are considerably more likely than men to be the victims of intimate partner homicide.[10] Again, those in marginalized communities are at greater risk.[11]

Victims of DV often consider divorce a last resort. Getting involved earlier in the relationship could lead to less abuse and fewer divorces. Addressing toxic traits early, before they become habitual and deeply entrenched, may give these relationships a better chance. Abuse is not an area to declare what happens within the home to be a private matter. It is not something that prayer and forgiveness will miraculously heal, particularly when the oppressor is unwilling to acknowledge the abusive behavior and end the oppression.

I encourage you to talk about DV in premarital counseling. When you speak or teach about marriage include disclaimers about abuse, describing it and how it manifests in relationships. If your church hosts or supports marriage retreats or seminars, make sure the content includes discussion and condemnation of abusive behavior. Have leaders mention DV in Sunday School and small group teachings. Churches must be willing to address the issue of

6. Goldstein, *Quincy Solution*, loc. 455.
7. Institute on Strangulation Prevention, *Let's Create Your Safety Plan*, 2.
8. Hernon and Tompkins, "Intimate Partner Homicide," 16.
9. NCADV, "Domestic Violence and Firearms," bullet point 5.
10. Hernon and Tompkins, "Intimate Partner Homicide," 2.
11. Resource Center on Domestic Violence, "Co-Occurrence of Child Abuse."

toxic and abusive behavior, making sure that all congregants know that it is unbiblical and unacceptable. This is hard but necessary work. The church must speak up because silence is complicity.

Protecting and caring for victims and survivors of abuse should never be predicated on whether a divorce has occurred or may happen in the future. This work cannot be conducted solely with a view toward reconciliation either. In his article about forcing forgiveness, Wilco de Vries, a research fellow at Duke Divinity School, stated that the proper response to injustice is not reconciliation, but repentance.[12] I heartily agree. If you believe that the one who has perpetrated harm is ready and willing to do the hard work of giving up power and control in the relationship and taking personal responsibility for the abusive attitudes, behaviors, and actions, you can use appendix E to guide you in assessing change over time.

---

12. De Vries, "Danger of Forcing Forgiveness."

14

Preaching, Teaching, and Training Leadership

DOMESTIC VIOLENCE CAN NO longer be a taboo topic in the church.[1] Victims want their faith leaders to understand abuse, denounce it from the pulpit, and address it in other areas of church life as well. Most churches offer a variety of programming options. Sunday School classes, small groups, women's groups, men's groups, youth and children's groups, Bible studies, seminars, weekend workshops, and other groups and special events are common. Many unordained individuals teach and/or provide leadership in faith-based spaces, which makes it necessary that both ordained clergy and lay leaders have knowledge of something that impacts such a large section of our population. Lay leaders are often ready and willing to assist but generally wait for the pastor to take a leadership initiative.[2]

It is vital that training take place and continue to impact not just those already serving in ministry roles, but also those who are preparing for any kind of church-related work in the future. In the portion of the CC&DV research for faith leaders, I asked about DV training. Thirty-six percent received no training about

1. Zust et al., "10-Year Study."
2. Homiak and Singletary, "Family Violence in Congregations," 34.

DV. Twenty-five percent had it mentioned in a course curriculum. Less than 20 percent had attended any kind of DV training event during seminary or college. The balance had encountered abuse in books, in talking with survivors, or in other experiences. The importance of what this research revealed was that those who engaged with DV training during seminary or college were also more likely to continue to get DV training after seminary or college.[3]

The concept of educating faith leaders about DV is greater than pastors and preaching, but that is where it starts. One survivor I spoke with mentioned how the pulpit sets the tone for the congregation, and I agree. How a pastor approaches the topic of DV informs any victims in the congregation whether it is safe to approach the pastor about abuse. Silence from the pulpit about abuse can become a roadblock for victims seeking treatment.[4] Sermons that show how to love others and not harm them are essential. Clear teaching about how physical, emotional, and verbal violence violates Scripture is necessary. Hearing this from the pulpit opens channels of communication for victims and survivors to speak to the pastoral staff with more confidence.

Church programming should address family life and advocate for nonviolence in all relationships.[5] Clergy have a role in shaping congregants' understanding of Scripture, including expectations for acceptable behavior.[6] One reason it is so important for victims to hear about the evil of abuse from church leadership is that it is not uncommon for abusers to use a sermon or church teaching about marriage to spread a DV culture at home. Certain aspects of religion can be used to justify and perpetuate abuse.[7] A message about the permanence of marriage, submission, forgiveness, reconciliation, or the duties of wives, without also discussing abuse and the responsibility of husbands to be respectful, loving, and kind to their wives, will cause damage. We want our preaching

3. Goertzen and Fox, "Response of Christian Faith."
4. Perilla, "Role of Churches," 2.
5. Homiak and Singletary, "Family Violence in Congregations," 22.
6. Shannon-Lewy and Dull, "Response of Christian Clergy," 649.
7. Simonič, "Power of Women's Faith," 4279.

to empower victims to incorporate what they hear from the pulpit into their daily lives, not to feel like sermons and other teachings will be weaponized against them.

Church teachings ought to include what Christ loving the church looks like. Preaching and other lessons can include discussions of healthy and toxic behaviors, describing how some behaviors display the Fruit of the Spirit in our lives, while others indicate the works of the flesh. Faith leaders can describe how abuse is the ongoing, willful tactics of power and control to subjugate another, and that toxic behavior is never Christlike. Let your congregants know that all forms of abuse are evidence of the abandonment of marriage vows and that God does not hold victims of abuse in bondage to destructive marriages.

It would be helpful to consider how sermons and other church teachings would sound to those who have experienced abuse. Will they find hope in the message, or will the sermon cause further pain? It is also helpful to consider whole-church ideals regarding marriage. One survivor told me about how her church applauded couples with lengthy marriages, knowing full well that at least one of the wives was in a harmful one. In this case, it was not a celebration of what was good and beautiful for many years but of what one woman endured endlessly because of the church's stance on no divorce for cases of abuse.

Victims and survivors of abuse have also been harmed at church through joking, or the anecdotes and illustrations used. When humor is used to make light of someone's plight, or when one gender or marginalized group is the brunt of the joke, it can cause emotional pain. The quip "if the barn needs painting, then paint it" is a mild example of humor at the expense of female appearance. It would be helpful to discourage biased and damaging stereotyped illustrations. This same concept should apply to men's groups, women's groups, and young adult or youth settings. Traumatized individuals want to feel safe and secure in our congregations, and not have to worry if the message or illustrations will **trigger** them. Victims and survivors work overtime trying to manage triggers, and it would bless them to know that church is a safe space.

Other topics used to silence victims and keep them in subjection, whether in the home or church, are suffering and forgiveness. Leonie Westenberg, a lecturer at Notre Dame University in Sydney, Australia, summarizes why that reasoning is problematic. Victims of abuse continue to endure harm, without a guarantee that their suffering will end the problem of evil behavior, and this one-sided mandate is placed on the victim while the perpetrator is excused.[8] Nancy Nason-Clark points out that spiritual language about forgiveness and second chances means that women of faith wait longer to seek help and are more likely to believe that the violence will end.[9] Forgiveness, however, does not require accepting the continued injustice of abuse, and it is good to keep in mind that any repentance must include turning away from destructive patterns.

It could be that faith leaders are hesitant to preach about DV due to concern that the topic will be difficult for the congregation. If the fear is hurting a victim of abuse, you can offer a trigger warning about difficult material by telling the congregation that you will be speaking about DV and that you understand that it may be triggering for some folks. If there is someone in your congregation who has had a particularly difficult situation, you may wish to speak to them in the week prior to the service just in case they need to stay home and/or catch the service online that week (if your church offers that option).

If pastors are fearful of offending perpetrators, then we must look carefully at why that is so. Churches cannot remain healthy and provide shelter for victims and survivors while protecting perpetrators. If the hesitancy to preach about abuse is to stifle a taboo topic to protect the institution of the church, we need to look no further than the Gospels to see an example of Jesus overturning the tables in the temple due to injustice (Matt 21:12). The Scriptures ask us to do right, seek justice, and defend the oppressed (Isa 1:17).

8. Westenberg, "When She Calls for Help," 8.
9. Nason-Clark et al., *Religion and Intimate Partner Violence*, 34.

In a recent sermon, Rev. Hannah Coe summed this up perfectly in stating that those who are concerned with the kingdom of God will be those who are concerned with justice.[10]

As much as victims and survivors want and need to hear about abuse from the pulpit, there are others who will disapprove. It could be that a family leaves the church over such words. There may be those who disagree and get angry. If this happens, take careful stock of who is upset over these words against DV. What do you know about the family? Does the spouse fit the profile of a victim of abuse? Do the children fit the profile of childhood domestic abuse victims? If there is any suspicion of DV in the family, check in with them, but be cautious in your interactions. Consider how you can carefully open communication with those who may need it.

Sermons and faith messages should include examples of how God has liberated the oppressed or provided a way of escape. Biblical evidence of escape from evil or disaster is present from cover to cover. God protected Noah from the flood. The Hebrew midwives lied to protect babies who would have been killed. Moses led the Israelites out of the bondage of Pharaoh. The spies who went to Jericho survived with the help of Rahab the prostitute. David fled when Saul sought to kill him. Old Testament prophets escaped wicked kings. Queen Esther's people escaped death through her acts of bravery. Mary and Joseph protected baby Jesus from death by leaving in the middle of the night. Jesus escaped the angry mob after his first sermon. An earthquake aided in the release of Paul and Silas from prison. And Paul got away as his disciples lowered him in a basket through a window in the city wall. Examples of escape are plentiful.

The CC&DV research asked faith leaders how often and how comfortable they were in speaking and preaching about DV. Forty-seven percent indicated that they were very comfortable preaching about DV, 43 percent were somewhat comfortable, and 10 percent were not at all comfortable. Education and awareness are the best way to gain comfort in speaking about abuse from the

---

10. Coe, "Act Justly."

pulpit. Despite these professed comfort levels, when limiting the responses to just pastors, 44 percent claimed they never preached about DV, and 39 percent did so just once or twice a year.[11] If congregants hear their pastors preach against DV, they will feel much safer about disclosing any abuse they live with at home.

As ministers or individuals serving in a lay leadership capacity, we are a conduit for God's revelation to others by the way we speak about these topics, answer hard questions, and dialogue about faith amid traumatic circumstances. Information about trauma and DV is both a prevention and recovery strategy that will minimize the occurrence of abuse and increase resilience. Keep in mind that abuse affects lives every day. Those experiencing DV need our compassion, support, and validation. They need to know that the people of God are concerned with their well-being. They need to know that we will take this seriously.

---

11. Goertzen and Fox, "Response of Christian Faith."

15

Women in Ministry and Church Leadership Are Vital in the Response to Abuse

SEVERAL FEMALE SURVIVORS OF abuse shared with me that even conservative churches were too liberal for their husbands. They could only attend extreme patriarchal churches in which women were second-class citizens or home churches where the abuser was the sole authority and only spiritual advisor for the family. These husbands expected blind obedience and demanded servitude. The women had little value and few rights. Religious patriarchy was a mechanism of power and oppression labeled as God's ideal. But in the wise words of Beth Barr, although the Bible was written in a patriarchal time, that doesn't make patriarchy a Christian concept.[1]

My interviews with survivors provided additional information about patriarchy in their homes. Some husbands punished their wives at home for daring to speak up in Sunday School. Even in strictly controlled settings, husbands accused them of trying to catch the eye of another man. Multiple husbands changed their minds about church attendance after the wedding, not giving their wives any choice. Even though they were married in the church,

---

1. Barr, *Making of Biblical Womanhood*, 36–37.

one husband subsequently claimed he hated God but neither would he allow his wife to attend church without him.

Stories such as this indicate why some women struggle to see themselves as God's beloved. They may have heard that women were not created in the image of God but in the image of man. Their own gifts and talents are not acknowledged, nor are they allowed to hear or experience God's calling in their own lives. Survivors have explained that in some churches, a husband or father stands between a woman and God. This completely disregards the individual priesthood of the believer. As the apostle Paul instructed Timothy, salvation is a personal decision, and each believer goes directly to God without the need for a mediator (1 Tim 2:5).

It is helpful when churches highlight and proclaim the stories that show the value of women in the Bible and female heroes of the faith. Preach and teach about Miriam, Rahab, Ruth, Abigail, Deborah, Jael, Huldah, Esther, Elizabeth, Anna, Mary, Lydia, Priscilla, Junia, Phoebe, and Eunice. Acknowledge the women who sang, judged, led, taught, worshiped, prayed, and prophesied. Outline their tales of bravery, strength, and dedication. There are also hundreds of examples of how women served in the early church. Examine the women through history who have made a difference in the life of the church. Women are important to God. It goes against Scripture to say otherwise. To quote Beth Barr once again, Jesus lived in a world that did not value the words of women yet chose a woman to be the first witness of his resurrection.[2] That is profound.

Seeing women in leadership, and hearing the value of women at church, begins to put the context of a woman's relationship with God back into order. Consider the overall message that your church portrays to those who attend. How are women treated? Do women hold any positions of authority in your congregation? Are women ordained as deacons or ministers? Are women welcomed in the pulpit? I encourage you to place women in visible leadership roles wherever you can. The sharing of power in congregations is one way to promote equality and alleviate the power differential

2. Barr, *Making of Biblical Womanhood*, 87.

in churches. Seeing that women in your church have value will let victims of abuse know that they have value.

Most victims of DV are female. Most pastors are male. That difference alone can make it hard for female victims and survivors to speak about what they have experienced, especially if the DV includes sexual abuse. Female victims of DV would often prefer to have a female pastor or faith leader with whom they can speak about the abuse. Training female clergy, lay leaders, chaplains, and counselors could be exactly the response to DV that churches need.

If your church or denomination does not include women in the pastorate, consider what lay leadership positions place women in your congregation within the visible reach of potential victims and survivors. Educate the women who lead small groups and Sunday School classes about abuse. Women who work with children and youth should also receive this education, as it can be a child that reveals something not quite right at home. The wives of pastors and other church leaders should be aware of the dynamics of toxic marriages and how to help those who may come to them for assistance. Without training on how to respond to abuse, it is possible to mishandle such situations.

This is not to say that it is only women who are helpful in cases of abuse. I have heard of cases where it was women who were the harshest and showed the least compassion to victims of abuse. The CC&DV research also revealed that some female respondents had the least supportive responses. The one response that stated it was not important to hold abusers accountable was from a female, the one response that female victims should be counseled to submit more was a female, and four females stated that church discipline for the *victim* was very important.[3]

Gender alone doesn't make a difference in the response to DV. Training regarding DV is essential for anyone in any kind of leadership position. Faith leaders have misunderstood, minimized, and dismissed the damage created by DV, causing victims to report that their clergy members were of little help.[4] In the CC&DV

3. Goertzen and Fox, "Response of Christian Faith."
4. Tracy, "Clergy Responses to Domestic Violence," 9.

survivor interviews, many spoke of the desire to see women in church leadership. One survivor mentioned how pastors at her church did not meet with women alone, so how would she ever be able to privately discuss the abuse she lived with? Another survivor disclosed the abuse to a male pastor and male elder, both of whom then sided with her abuser.

A lack of access to a female faith leader is even more problematic and intimidating when the alternative is for a female victim to meet with two male leaders in the church. Congregational studies show that only 14 percent of congregations are led by women, with mainline, Black Protestant, and Jewish synagogues being the most likely to be led by women, and evangelical Protestant and Roman Catholic congregations being least likely.[5] Churches that have women who serve in leadership were associated with more efforts to support DV victims in their congregations and communities.[6]

A **coordinated community response** is ideal in the efforts to create a congregation that reduces DV and maximizes support. Assess your congregation for women who work in capacities that could be part of a community response. The medical field, social work, counseling or therapy, mentoring, crisis shelters, employment agencies, food banks, local helping entities, and organizations that serve marginalized communities are all possibilities. Consider how your church can utilize these connections to serve those affected by DV. Can you coordinate or partner in a way that does not violate victim and survivor confidentiality? Which individuals have the capacity to be involved in your church's efforts? Set up occasional meetings to ensure that your church's response is adequate and ready to serve when necessary. If your church is smaller, more rural, or doesn't have these connections within your own congregation, can you partner with another church that does?

We live in a fallen world where difficult things happen even to the best people. Sometimes life is just a mystery. The idea that God does not give us more than we can handle is not in Scripture. The truth is that sometimes we do have more than we can handle

---

5. Chaves et al., *Congregations in 21st Century*, 36.
6. Zust et al., "Evangelical Christian Pastors," 678.

alone—not just in cases of DV but also in a devastating cancer diagnosis, extreme loss due to natural disasters, or the death of a child. However, God promises to never leave us or forsake us (Heb 13:5). We must promote the message that God is near to the brokenhearted (Ps 34:18) as we share God's love for the wounded in our areas of ministry, whether that is in a professional context or as a lay leader in a local congregation or another faith-based ministry.

In word and deed, churches can stand against violence, protect the violated, and affirm that women have inherent worth as daughters divinely created in the image of God. When they are beloved at church, they will come to believe that there is a God who loves them unconditionally despite the abuse they may experience at home. Consider what your congregation can do to help victims and survivors find safety in your church and among its leadership. I encourage you to take inventory to see what already works in your congregation regarding DV response, and what could use improvement. Contemplate where your congregation can place women in leadership and train them to recognize and respond to DV so that they are ready to support the recovery of those who have experienced abuse. Appendix D can help with that.

Almost every time I speak about abuse, survivors seek me out to share their stories. One time it was the adult son of a victim, who talked to me about his mother who was still living in abuse. On multiple occasions, after speaking about my personal experiences as a DV survivor, I have heard from elderly women that they experienced abuse as a child, or in their marriage, but never felt safe enough to talk about it to anyone at church. Each time I hear a story like that it grieves me that these women have carried this pain by themselves for five or six decades, without ever hearing about abuse at church until I shared my story. Talking about DV openly and making these conversations accessible to victims and survivors will make a difference. It will grant them the grace to begin to heal.

16

How to Respond to Domestic Violence

FIRST AND FOREMOST, IT is important to possess an understanding of DV in order to respond faithfully and not cause more anguish or put victims in harm's way. Let victims know that you care. Assure them that you believe them, that this is not their fault, and that no one deserves such behavior. Affirm the courage it took to speak up about the abuse. Help them comprehend that abuse is a pattern of behaviors that tend to get worse instead of better. Assume the best about the victim. The victim is less likely to be someone seeking to leave the marriage at the first sign of trouble, and more likely someone who has poured an immense amount of time and dedication into trying to hold the relationship together.

Do not blame a victim or ask for proof. Do not judge them for how they responded to the abuse, or pressure them to make immediate decisions. Do not go to a victim's abuser to verify conversations you've had in confidence with the victim. Pastoral counseling has its place, but remember that couples counseling in cases of abuse is contraindicated. Know your limitations. Thoughtful leaders surround themselves with people who are experts in their individual fields and know when to refer to someone who has more education and experience with the given situation. Have a list of resources and referrals ready to offer when someone discloses DV to you.

Victims and survivors want empathetic listening more than they need advice. Talk with victims in a safe space and assure confidentiality unless there's an issue that requires mandatory reporting. See appendix A for information on clergy as mandated reporters. Consider the safety of the victim and any children. If you suspect they are in danger, you can express that concern. Gently ask open-ended questions. If you think a crime has been committed or if there are lethality risks, such as strangulation and weapons, consider the need to engage the authorities and apply for protective orders.

After considering safety, connect the victim to resources. You may want to start by getting the local family violence shelter involved, or having the victim call the National DV Hotline. You can request information, but to initiate services, the service provider will need to speak to the survivor directly. If a survivor is worried or nervous or hesitant to make the phone call, offer to sit with them while they do.

An adult victim is not required to report abuse. If it is reported, it must be in the victim's own timing. Support the capacity of the individual to make the best decision for a particular situation. There may be reasons that someone is hesitant to report abuse to authorities. Some individuals and groups have troubled relationships with law enforcement which makes reporting abuse a difficult choice. There have been times when authorities arrested the victim because the abuser claimed that she started it. Obviously, that helps no one, especially the children.

Jesus supported the spiritual and physical well-being of the people he healed. Caring for the tangible needs of those we minister to is another way to show them God's love. Does the victim need assistance from your church's benevolence fund? What necessities exist, and are there bills to be paid? Are there physical injuries that medical personnel should attend to? Does the person need access to housing? DV is a leading cause of homelessness for women and children.[1] High numbers of survivors have difficulty securing adequate, affordable housing after separating from their abuser.[2] The reduction in the standard of living falls much heavier on women and children than it does on men.

Evaluate your congregation for individuals and families that can offer various forms of support—meals, clothing, childcare, household needs, car repairs, employment, help with budgeting, court accompaniment, and friendship. There should be services in your area that provide for some of these needs, but consider the capacity of your congregation to fill these areas if safety permits. Find people in the congregation who can be a part of a support network. Pair the victim with those who will provide long-term companionship. A congregation can be a rich source of aid and a community to support and invest in the lives of those recovering after DV. Through this, victims and survivors will understand that they are not alone.

Pray aloud for those affected by abuse, violence, and assault from the pulpit and in group settings—not by name, of course, because that breaks confidentiality, but as a collective group. For example, in my first chapel in seminary one of the professors prayed for the "single mom who struggles" and in that prayer, I felt seen. That professor didn't even know me, and yet acknowledged my struggles through his prayer. When a year and a half later I took his preaching course, I let him know how much that meant to me.

Examine personal bias about victims of DV. Be willing to have difficult conversations. Define words and situations clearly. Give space for Sunday School and small groups to discuss the topic. Have relationship discussions with youth and young adults. Consult appendix C if you plan to talk about DV in premarital counseling. Consider offering space for a support group if there is a need for one. Share and recommend this book to other faith leaders and churches. Humbly listen to the voices of those with lived experience. Ask what they may need from you and your

1. National Coalition for the Homeless, "Domestic Violence and Homelessness," 1.
2. Moulding et al., "Rethinking Women's Mental Health," 1069.

church. Be willing to admit prior shortcomings. We must create justice *with* survivors and not just for them.

The Psalms are a great place to start when working with victims of abuse. In the Psalms, we see the Lord as a refuge for the oppressed and a stronghold in times of trouble (Ps 9:9). God sees the trouble of the afflicted and considers their grief (Ps 10:14). God listens to cries for help (Ps 22:24). God defends the weak and upholds the cause of the poor and the oppressed and delivers them from the wicked (Ps 82:3–4). The Lord works righteousness and justice for the oppressed (Ps 103:6). God heals the brokenhearted and binds their wounds (Ps 147:3). Many Psalms describe deep weariness, something victims and survivors can identify closely with. God is there when even we cannot see or feel the Divine presence.

Know that there is a difference between a survivor who is honestly and sincerely trying to get faith leaders to understand the nature of the abuse in the home and a perpetrator who is using blame, manipulation, and character assassination to get faith leaders to take sides against the survivor. It requires discernment. It requires standing in solidarity with the injured party (who is often powerless in the situation) and not tolerating the acts of the abuser (who will often be using power and status to control the situation). It requires understanding that there is no neutrality in trying to stay neutral. In his speech to accept the Nobel Prize, holocaust survivor Elie Wiesel said that we must take sides because our neutrality serves the oppressor and never the one being oppressed.[3]

Even if submission, suffering, and reconciling with an abusive spouse are not regular topics in your church, it is still necessary to call out the structural oppression that results from such doctrines. Pastoral care must interrupt the pathways that lead to dismissing the gravity of DV. Not doing so continues the cycle of violence and allows the next generation to establish environments of control and deception, where sin hides, and where oppression continues. A culture of DV is an environment where prevailing

---

3. Wiesel, "Nobel Prize Speech," para. 9.

attitudes normalize, trivialize, and excuse both physical and non-physical forms of DV.

Although awareness has increased over the last four decades, and advocates are making progress with prevention and intervention efforts, DV culture is still common. Domestic violence culture blames victims for the abuse they endure and clings to remnants of patriarchal assumptions about women and children being the commodities of men. It includes a variety of issues, including how victims might report DV to authorities, how legislative and judicial systems handle abuse, how the media portrays it, and how institutions of faith respond.

Regarding those who have perpetrated harm, you have probably heard it said that hurt people hurt people. That can be true, but it doesn't have to be. Those who have experienced childhood abuse are also more likely to experience future violence, perpetrate violence, engage in substance misuse, and have more limited educational attainment and job opportunities.[4] But it cannot be an excuse because not every child abuse victim grows up to perpetuate harm. Many do not engage in inflicting intentional pain on others, having decided that the abuse stops with them. They make determined efforts toward healing and do not engage in toxic behavior.

It is important that you know that few perpetrators will want to observe healthy boundaries, take full responsibility, or desire ongoing accountability. They may be upset with you for supporting restraining orders or accompanying the victim to court. Do not excuse their behavior. Don't assume this is just an anger problem. Yes, abusers use fits of anger and rage against their victims, but the anger usually ends there. Many abusers have no problem controlling their anger when there are witnesses, especially high-profile witnesses like pastors, police, attorneys, and judges. For those, the abuser can stay calm. But remember that the victim sees a completely different side.

Keep in mind that bystanders can be at risk from abusers as well. Know that when toxic behavior spills out of the home onto bystanders and witnesses, including congregants and pastors, you

---

4. CDC, "About Child Abuse and Neglect."

are seeing the potential for additional harm. Studies show that about 20 percent of victims in DV disturbances and homicides are bystanders.[5] Know that abuse can be fatal. Even if there is a protective order. Even if the perpetrator is believed to be a man of God who holds a position of church leadership. Risk to all congregants is why DV policy in churches is so important. It protects victims but ultimately also protects the rest of the congregation as well. Church policy is further addressed in another chapter, and there are policy suggestions in appendix B.

The victim and perpetrator should not remain in the same congregation as this would put the victim at further risk for harm. From prior conversations, I knew that it was DV survivors who often had to leave their churches, so the CC&DV faith leader survey asked respondents if they believed it was important to remove the abuser from the congregation. The faith leaders indicated that it was either somewhat important (45 percent) or very important (34 percent) to remove the abuser from the church. Respondents varied on the issue of church discipline for the abuser with 38 percent believing it was very important, 39 percent believing it was somewhat important, and 24 percent believing it was not important. A whopping 92 percent believed it was very important to hold the abuser accountable. With these responses, it is interesting that it is still the survivors who usually have to leave their church homes.

In another survey question, faith leaders were asked what percentage of abusers they believed could permanently change their behavior and become non-abusive. It is interesting to note that about half of the responding faith leaders put this number between 10–20 percent and almost all respondents indicated 30 percent or less. Even these faith leaders seemed to think that lasting change is rare. If perpetrators are willing to accept your help, then assess the situation, and help them separately from their victims. There must agreement to stop engaging in all forms of harm and put concerted efforts into attitudes and behaviors of nonviolence. Professional counseling and intervention will be necessary.

5. Smith et al., "Intimate Partner Homicide," 461.

HOW TO RESPOND TO DOMESTIC VIOLENCE

There is an urgency in how we respond to DV. When informed about abuse and trauma, churches are a natural entity to offer healing to the hurting. We can deliver an accurate depiction of the Living, Breathing, Caring, Almighty God. We have an obligation to frame the hope that is within us in a way that conveys it to others. Victims and survivors of abuse long for that hope. They need that hope. We can help them rediscover it.

17

Helping Survivors Find Healing

BASED ON CURRENT DV statistics, victims and survivors are sitting in your pews. Keep in mind the high incidence of DV. Remember that the rates of DV in religious families are similar to the general population.[1] They may not be talking about it for a variety of reasons, but they are there. The culture of your faith community will make the difference in whether they feel safe enough to speak of what they have experienced. We can embody the hope of the gospel through our response. Our actions and concerns should consider safety first and then follow up with additional pastoral care for the victim and any children.

    Survivors need to know and feel that God cares for them in their time of greatest need. The sacred truth of knowing that God is concerned with their pain and suffering can aid in the growth and healing process. Victims need us to be attentive to their situations. Survivors who are starting over in life need an extra measure of grace as they adjust to their new normal. They all need to hear prayers that include healing for the oppressed and messages from their faith leaders that DV is a violation of Scripture. They should feel our willingness to walk through dark valleys alongside them, as their broken hearts and wounded spirits heal. They

---

1. Westenberg, "When She Calls for Help," 2–3.

want you to be an ally who listens without judgment and respects their boundaries.

Some victims and survivors don't know what to do with God anymore, which is understandable considering the many examples shared in this book. It helps to present God as a loving being, a caregiver, and a healer of wounds. This presentation of a gracious God helps them sort out notions of the angry, vindictive, controlling God their abuser may have used against them. When the church speaks out against DV and corrects harmful theology, victims and survivors will be able to untangle their confusion about religious topics. As we show care and kindness, we encourage victims and survivors to consider whom they believe God to be and how faith is a part of healing.

Those in need of liberation from abuse view the Bible through a different lens. It is the lens of the struggle for survival—physical survival, emotional survival, and spiritual survival. If you feel they are hesitant to trust you, don't take that personally. Their trust in their partner, and often in others, was literally betrayed and destroyed. Even after they are free from daily DV, survivors deal with the aftermath of the trauma. It would not be unusual to struggle to trust again.

Embarrassment about marrying someone who turned out to be abusive or shame regarding not getting out of the abuse sooner are often present. Fear of judgment by church leadership for separating or seeking a divorce is frequent. Post-traumatic stress, anxiety, and depression are common. Don't be surprised if the survivor needs to take a step back from church life to regroup and recharge.

They may be trying to deal with damage control. Many of the survivors I spoke with mentioned that their abusive spouse started a **smear campaign** to destroy their reputation and separate them from any support. One survivor learned that her abuser was playing audio and videos of her breakdown to their church's small group members, a clear demonstration of his attempt to sabotage her reputation among the congregation. Another learned that her husband claimed she was having affairs, and all the while he was openly living with his girlfriend and still attending the same church.

Something to be aware of is the substantial grief and loss experienced by victims and survivors of abuse. They married with a dream of happily ever after, but their spouse delivered a dreadful nightmare. They are grieving the loss of what they hoped would be. They are grieving the loss of time. They may be grieving the fact that children have been born into toxic homes. They could be grieving emotional or geographic separations because of isolation. Additionally, they could be grieving the loss of family and friends who have deserted them in their time of need.

A church family is so important to those navigating loss. As those who experience a death, devastating illness, or natural disaster know, having that church family surround them with love and care makes an immense difference. Survivors of DV experience grief in similar ways as those mourning a death, except that the losses of survivors are often not acknowledged or understood by those around them.[2] Knowing this, you can be attentive to those who grieve after abuse, keeping in mind that the grieving process takes time.

The survivors interviewed for my CC&DV research mentioned the need for congregational support numerous times. They need not just crisis intervention, but also long-term support. They want churches to be involved in **safety planning** and to have resources on hand that they might not otherwise know about. They want the church to have connections to therapists, social workers, and organizations trained to assist in cases of DV. There is a shortage of ongoing support systems and support groups for DV, especially in faith communities. However, when survivors receive support from their faith community, it provides a sense of security and belonging.[3]

Caregiving skills can aid in the development of relationships that heal and empower. In supportive caregiving, there is an ability to stabilize, nurture, and guide those in our care, at their own pace. We can inspire growth and promote self-determination while we encourage them to discover their strengths and become active participants in change. Allow them the dignity of directing their own care based on their needs. It is best to not rush victims or survivors

---

2. Messing et al., "Intimate Partner Violence and Grief," 31.
3. Simonič, "Power of Women's Faith," 4289.

into making decisions or to make the decisions for them. Abusive spouses have already controlled their whole existence, and having yet one more person take control of their lives is not helpful.

Some of the most useful skills in providing care to victims and survivors are based on the ministry of presence: personal contact, listening, silence, empathy, sympathy, and asking open-ended questions. Allowing them to share their thoughts, fears, and their pain validates their experience. When they trust us with this information, we need to hold it as a sacred encounter and be worthy of that trust. Part of the ministry of presence also includes knowing what not to do. Victims who have been physically and sexually assaulted may need some distance. There should be careful use of personal space and seating arrangements. Ask for permission before touching or offering a hug. Integrity should be foremost in our interactions with survivors.

Faith leaders can stand in solidarity with those who struggle in abusive homes. We can help survivors rebuild after leaving DV and seeking safety. We can identify those who are struggling, check in on those who are hurting, and help those in need. Victims and survivors of abuse need to hear their pastors, especially male clergy, condemn abuse and acknowledge what victims have experienced. Female victims need to know that male faith leaders will stand against DV rather than require them to submit to it. Men must call other men as allies against abuse.[4]

As the second greatest command, loving our neighbors as ourselves demonstrates the love of God. Our Christian character is visible in our love for others. Even if we have the gift of prophecy, or have faith to move mountains, without love we are nothing (1 Cor 13:2). Part of our sacred calling is being a light in a world that is dark with grief, loss, and disappointment. Being a light means consistently shining God's love on heartbroken humans and living out God's love in relationships with victims and survivors, as we partner with them in mending their worlds.

It is possible for life to be good, even in the midst of adversity, because God is good. God's goodness makes joy attainable even in

---

4. CDC, "About Intimate Partner Violence," 2.

deep pain. When God is for us, who can be against us (Rom 8:31)? Yet those who have experienced abuse may see little that is good, and when they don't see goodness from those who claim to be followers of Christ, the tragedy is deep. The people of God must step up and demonstrate God's love and peace. Survivors who engage with faith and spirituality while coping with DV retain a greater sense of purpose and meaning.[5]

Most people are resilient, and recovery is possible when the environment is conducive to mitigating past trauma. As members of the body of Christ, we can serve the way Jesus did, feeding those who are hungry, healing those who are sick, and confronting the injustice around us. The church has the tools to produce hope in the lives of those oppressed by DV. What victims and survivors encounter in houses of worship makes a difference in their ability to cling to that hope. We can lead with genuine concern for victims and survivors of abuse and demonstrate that caring for the wounded is of extraordinary importance.

Helping survivors find wholeness and healing after DV empowers them to develop inner strengths, which in turn allows some who have escaped abuse to become advocates for the benefit of others. Seasoned survivors are especially helpful to those newly out of the abuse because they can provide strength from one who has been there. You may even wish to ask permission of one who has healed from abuse to speak with those who are new to the discovery of abuse in their lives. I can personally attest to the power of community and kindred spirits among survivors of DV, and the healing that comes from that community.

The church ought to be a place that heals parched souls. Based on the many accounts I have shared, it is understandable that many victims and survivors of DV struggle to participate in organized religion. With awareness and education about DV and empathy and concern for those who have experienced abuse, we can create safe spaces in our houses of faith. But this must be an intentional focus on the part of faith leaders. We must take abuse seriously if we want to address the impact of DV in our communities.

5. Simonič, "Power of Women's Faith," 4295.

18

Why It Matters and Putting It All into Practice

DOMESTIC VIOLENCE CAN AFFECT your entire congregation. From the effects of DV during pregnancy to the consequences of hearing and seeing any form of abuse during childhood, to teens and young adults getting into abusive dating relationships, to the anguish of experiencing abuse as an adult, to the magnitude of elder adults having hidden the abuse they lived with because their generation didn't talk of such things—DV can literally impact everyone in a church community. Those who haven't experienced it personally are probably aware of someone who has.

It is typical to think that our own congregations are untouched by DV. A Lifeway study in 2018 indicated that pastors were more likely to think abuse happened elsewhere, outside their churches.[1] But statistics tell another story and indicate the reality of abuse within our pews. Those who experience abuse may not be able to name and describe what they are living with as DV, especially if there is a history of minimizing its reality and severity. Not describing it as abusive doesn't mean it's not abuse. It just means the victim doesn't yet have the vocabulary to accurately describe what is happening. This is true of faith leaders as well. With

1. Lifeway Research, *Domestic and Gender-Based Violence*, 21–23.

comprehensive DV education, church leaders can help victims and survivors of abuse fully recognize and address what has happened.

Church leadership should always take advantage of further training, or an opportunity to speak with an advocate about DV for guidance on the best way to handle cases of abuse. Imagine the change that churches could create across the nation and around the world if congregational leaders chose awareness and education so that churches could respond quickly and appropriately to situations of DV. The impact on improved mental and physical health alone are reasons to pursue further training; but of course, this impacts spiritual health as well.

It is important that we help provide the appropriate vocabulary to our congregants, which is why congregational training on DV is vital. It is why the glossary at the end of this book is a valuable resource. Most pastors do not receive DV training in seminary or college and have not attended such training since. Counselors, chaplains, and lay leaders may also lack knowledge on this subject. Gaps in DV education may be due to a lack of information about seminars, a perceived lack of time to engage in training, or due to a perception that DV training isn't needed. On the contrary, such training is vital and will save lives. It is worth your time and effort.

Domestic homicide is the tragic ending that no congregation wants to face. I spoke with two mothers who had both lost daughters in this way. If you ever find your congregation facing this tragedy, stay connected with the victim's families, including parents, children, and siblings. Understand that domestic murder is a complicated grief and loss with no time limit. Don't pressure them about forgiveness for the accused. Don't suggest the victim was to blame or at fault in any way. Don't assume that the perpetrator, someone you may have believed to be a man of God, is innocent. This is why it is vital that we do not ignore or cover up signs of abuse. It is important that you address difficult and uncomfortable topics and create a congregation that is concerned about DV. Do pursue justice. Do support those affected.

In my research, survivors wanted the whole church to have the education to define DV correctly and know the signs of it.

They also wanted the **victim blaming** and the minimization of the abuse to end. They want their pastors to listen to the experiences of the abuse without judgment, especially the historically marginalized voices: women, people of color, immigrants and refugees, the LGBTQ+ community, people in recovery after substance use, those with disabilities, and those without financial resources. Each of these groups faces greater barriers to receiving assistance. If you or your church do not have the capacity to provide aid to those in a marginalized community, connect them to those who will help.

Because victims and survivors need access to many resources and services, it is wise for faith leaders to work with a team of people to help as needed. One of the best ways to do this is by connecting with the local family violence program and shelter. Know how far away it is and about the services they offer. A pastor can get to know the director and take a tour of the facility so there is a mental image of where to refer victims. Knowing about the local shelter means that clergy are more likely to make referrals.

If the shelter has brochures, take some to display at the church in both prominent (foyer, offices) and less prominent (restrooms) locations. I always feel encouraged when I go into a church I've never attended and see domestic violence brochures in the women's restroom. Even if a victim doesn't take one home, the presence of those brochures tells her that the church has thought through the situation and cares enough to display a helpful message to those who are in toxic relationships. The CC&DV research results indicated that only 21 percent of respondents said their church displayed brochures about DV.

I also asked faith leaders about their relationship with their local family violence shelter. Only 12 percent had met the director and toured the shelter. Less than 4 percent had received training from the shelter. Having the shelter provide training to church staff, deacons, or even the entire congregation is a great way to receive up-to-date, comprehensive information about DV. The more people trained, the more your congregation can help. Your church may want to consider giving financial or in-kind donations to the shelter as well. If your church is in a rural area without a shelter, consider what other services you can access in your state.

A full 96 percent of faith leaders who responded to the CC&DV survey believed that the church has a role in intervening in cases of abuse.[2] However, there is a scarcity of abuse prevention in churches. Although many churches are starting to address child protection policies, few have considered policies on the topic of DV. Due to the high number of families affected by abuse, it is time to start addressing policy in this area as well. It would be wise for churches to create a plan regarding DV before there is a need for that plan. A good way to do this is to have a written DV policy.

Appendix B includes a sample church policy. As part of my work as an intern with the Center for Church and Community Impact, I created this template for addressing DV in the church. You may use it as a guide in creating a policy that fits your congregation's needs. Some denominational bodies already have policies regarding how their clergy should handle abuse. Self-governing churches with greater local autonomy and less denominational oversight may not have such policies to guide the church's response. Whichever category fits your church, please consider establishing a DV policy in the near future. Members of a congregation who have received DV training can provide collaboration with DV service providers and help create policies and procedures for responding to abuse that integrate with church structure while empowering victims and protecting the congregation.[3]

When a congregation discovers abuse within its midst, there should already be protocols in place for assuring the safety of victims, protecting their autonomy, and referring them to local DV services. Such a policy would assure proper care for the individuals and make sure that victims and their children are safe. My research showed that about a quarter of the responding faith leaders attended churches that had a DV policy, but most of those were unwritten, while only 4 percent had a written policy in place.

---

2. Goertzen and Fox, "Response of Christian Faith."
3. Houston-Kolnik et al., "Overcoming the 'Holy Hush,'" 150.

WHY IT MATTERS AND PUTTING IT ALL INTO PRACTICE

Forty-one percent did not have a DV policy at their church, and 34 percent were unsure if the church had any policy.

As leaders, we must faithfully represent God in our ministries. We must live into that ministry in the way that Jesus would—by tending to the least of these. The way we live out our calling might very well be what draws a survivor who is struggling after the abuse back to church, or what pushes that person away from ever reconnecting with a faith community. The church can be a source of comfort, warmth, security, and protection for survivors of DV, but only with education and awareness of the destructive nature of abuse. Without a strong understanding of DV, faith leaders might inadvertently do more harm than good.

Let us each evaluate the efforts we have undertaken to end abuse and protect those affected by it. We can address the issues of power, control, and dominance that lead to abusive behaviors in the home. We can provide support and encouragement to those starting over after significant trauma. We can partner together to increase awareness and respond faithfully. We can make the effort to invest in the lives of adult congregants, and also our children and youth so that we break the generational chain of abuse. I concluded my academic research article with a question regarding what portion of the message about educating faith leaders would encourage them to engage with the topic of DV in their church.[4] I ask you to consider the same.

As you put all this knowledge into practice, do it with an open heart and mind. Be willing to challenge the status quo in how the church responds to abuse. Stand up against harmful, victim-blaming actions and toxic behavior. Change the narratives within your field of influence. Be the Good Samaritan and render aid when others do not. While others pass by, be the one who stops to care for the wounded and helps them see their value in the kingdom of God.

I make myself available to the victims and survivors in my acquaintance because I have heard multiple times that there are few they can talk to. While I am always happy to help, it grieves

---

4. Goertzen and Fox, "Response of Christian Faith."

me that there are churches scattered across our country that are not able to help those hurting after experiencing DV. If the issue is education and awareness, confusion about the nature of abuse, or uncertainty about what victims and survivors face in their homes and in their churches, I hope this book has helped. Creating change in our communities requires an effort that will take years. We must start now.

It is essential that we walk life's journey with survivors, include them in fellowship, and demonstrate God's love to them. Jesus' ministry focused on providing good news, delivering the captives, and proclaiming the Lord's favor (Luke 4:18). I cannot think of anything more appropriate to describe a ministry to victims and survivors of DV. May we act justly, love mercy, and walk humbly with our God in doing so (Mic 6:8). And may we always take it seriously. Amen and amen.

19

Back to the Victim Case Study

KELLI WASN'T SURE SHE could carry the burden alone for much longer. The abuse was getting worse, and she didn't know what to do. She was scared. Scared of the violent outbursts and scared of the gun under his pillow at night. She was worried about how Dalton would treat the children if she separated, but she was also worried about the effect on the children if she stayed in their current tumultuous situation. The church they attended for a short time had not been supportive after the one domestic issue they knew about. No one on the pastoral staff had ever reached out to her to see if she was okay.

Although she didn't realize it yet, Kelli had experienced every form of abuse imaginable. Her health was beginning to deteriorate. She was physically and emotionally exhausted. She was on-call for the petty needs of a selfish, angry husband 24/7/365. She was chronically sleep deprived because he wouldn't allow her to sleep if he wasn't sleeping first. The one time she tried to attend a women's Bible study at church was a big mistake. The retribution experienced for that one night made it unwise for her to ever try it again.

But something had changed. A friend had given her a book that helped her recognize what she was living with. Things were finally making sense, and she was starting to gain clarity. It was becoming evident that Kelli would need to summon the courage to reach out for support on how to handle the abuse and what to do next. When Kelli reached out for help, it wasn't to a church or a pastor. It was to an old friend who lived out of town. This friend immediately urged her to seek local help. The verbal affirmations and emotional support from that first person gave her the courage to reach out to a second out-of-town friend who helped with safety planning.

Somehow it seemed safer to start with old friends who were not local. The love, concern, and acceptance she felt from them helped her tell someone nearby, and that person got her the phone number of the nearest domestic violence shelter and gave her gas money to get there. As Kelli realized that a little support network was forming, she gained the confidence to take the next steps toward a future without violence. It wasn't going to be easy, and she continued to worry about safety and finances, but she began to feel something new—she began to feel hope.

Alphabetical Glossary of Domestic Violence Terms

The glossary is meant to be an extensive, yet practical resource for those who have not engaged with in-depth training on the issue of domestic violence (DV), and a supplemental resource for those who have.

#ChurchToo—A social movement to bring awareness to sexual abuse and harassment within the context of a church. Although this often refers to clergy sexual assault, some victims of DV have been revictimized by a church when a pastoral authority takes advantage of the victim's vulnerability, which demonstrates a clear example of clergy sexual assault.

#MaybeHeDoesntHitYou—A social movement designed to bring awareness to the fact that abuse is far more than physical injury. It describes many types of verbal and emotional manipulation used to control the victim. It opens our eyes to the ways that control, abuse, and nonphysical injury happen in relationships.

#MeToo—A social movement against sexual abuse and harassment. Sexual abuse and harassment can occur in dating relationships or between acquaintances but can also occur within the context of marriage. Realizing the high incidence of sexual assault in marriage is necessary for those working with DV survivors who identify with faith and spirituality due to sexual abuse being a large part of the abuse they experience.

ALPHABETICAL GLOSSARY OF DOMESTIC VIOLENCE TERMS

#WhyIStayed—A social movement to bring awareness to why victims often stay in abusive relationships. Society, including faith communities, has often blamed and shamed victims, required that victims stay in violent relationships, and refused to provide resources and support that could help victims live safely. The honest answers of those who have stayed in abuse will open your eyes to what they have experienced and how hard it can be to leave an abusive relationship.

Advocates—Those trained to help victims of DV, through support and practical assistance. Pastors and faith leaders can advocate by actively seeking knowledge and awareness of the tactics of abuse, clearly speaking out against the sin of abuse, believing victims, and supporting survivors. Churches advocate for victims when they engage allies, provide resources, and refer out to other service providers. Advocacy happens when churches model equality, participate in prevention efforts, hold abusers accountable, and promote policies that support victims and survivors.

Baiting—Purposeful actions or comments designed to hurt, antagonize, or upset the victim in such a way that provokes a response. Perpetrators will bait their victims, trying to force them to break down or erupt, and respond negatively. It is not unheard of to provoke the victim to the point of physical response (which would be a defensive mechanism on the part of the victim and not an abusive one). The perpetrator can then use the provoked response against the victim, to make them appear unsettled and harmful. Baiting the victim is one tactic used by abusers in court-related proceedings to blame the victim in front of the authority of the court. Perpetrators will also use this to damage the reputation of the victim within the church by baiting the victim and then pointing to any overflow of emotion as ungodly.

Batterer—Another word for the oppressor, abuser, or perpetrator of violence. Someone who dominates, controls, and abuses another person.

ALPHABETICAL GLOSSARY OF DOMESTIC VIOLENCE TERMS

Battering Intervention and Prevention Program (BIPP)—Formal training, sometimes required by the courts, that educates and holds abusers accountable by teaching skills of nonviolence and challenging the attitudes and ideas rooted in coercive control. Most pastors do not have this type of professional training to handle the perpetrator on their own. If a pastor does attempt to engage in assisting the perpetrator, know that this is a long-term commitment of required accountability. Do not attempt to reconcile the victim and abuser while this work is in process. It is best to engage with such work outside the church environment so that the victim and abuser are not together in the same worship space.

Blame shifting—This happens when, instead of owning up to poor behavior, the abuser places blame on the victim, on work, on alcohol, on illness, etc. It is an emotionally abusive tactic to shift responsibility away from the perpetrator and onto the victim or other circumstances. Churches engage in shifting the blame onto victims when they ask what victims did to cause the abuse, if victims have prayed about the situation, or why victims weren't submissive. When a church engages in blaming the victim for the abusive behaviors, it allows the abuse to continue instead of addressing the real issue. On the other hand, if a church blames the victim for staying in the abuse, it excuses the societal systems that make it difficult for the victim to leave. The preferred response is accountability for poor behavior and support systems and safety for those subjected to abuse.

Boundaries—Describes a limit for how close a person will allow another person to get within a relationship. Boundaries in relationships help couples determine what is comfortable and not comfortable for each of them. Abuse violates boundaries, but in a healthy relationship, partners respect each other's boundaries. The church violates boundaries when using biblical texts to give ownership of a person's body over to the other spouse who then sees that as permission to perpetrate harm. Pastors and faith leaders should make sure of their own healthy boundaries before discussing boundaries in the lives of other people. A victim of abuse may be particularly vulnerable, and it is necessary to maintain professional boundaries within the pastoral care context so that the victim is not revictimized by a person of authority inside the church.

BROKEN HOMES—An outdated term, unfortunately still used to describe a family in which a divorce had occurred. It is important to remember that it is abuse, not divorce, that breaks a home. This term is degrading to those who have experienced abuse and/or divorce, and churches ought to refrain from using it, or use it only in the context of describing that it is the abuse that breaks the home, and not the separation or divorce. It is also important that it is not insinuated that those who have experienced abuse are broken in any way. The language we use can make or break our conversations with those who are hurting and seeking recovery after the trauma of abuse.

BYSTANDERS—In a situation of DV, this is a person who gets dragged into the conflict whether there was the intention to get involved or not. Police officers, clergy, relatives, friends, and coworkers are examples of bystanders who might witness or become involved in an altercation. It is important to know that bystanders can be unintended victims of injury or homicide in these cases. Please use caution, especially when a weapon might be involved. Safety planning may be of use in situations of uncertainty.

CHILDHOOD DOMESTIC ABUSE—The traumatizing effects on children include anxiety, depression, anger, fear, aggression, and antisocial behaviors. Learning and academic performance can be impacted as well. Childhood domestic abuse may increase truancy, running away, addiction, date rape, and teen pregnancy. Behavioral issues may reflect back to the conflict in the home. This is important information for church leaders working with children and teens. We can literally change the future of the next generation by addressing DV in our own towns, the nation, and around the world.

CHURCH RESPONSE—A church's decision to name and confront abuse through support for the victim, or to perpetuate DV through lack of awareness or negligence. A church injures victims when it minimizes the abuse by describing it as a conflict or disagreement instead of naming it for what it really is. When faith leaders respond with a lack of concern, victims feel devalued by the faith community. Sometimes an abuser will use church involvement to establish an alliance and thereby minimize the consequences of poor behavior. All clergy and lay leadership should be aware of the tactics of abuse and be mindful of manipulation. A church responds faithfully when it engages in education, provides awareness to leaders or congregants, creates DV policy, and supports those harmed by abuse. Congregations that are informed about DV will understand their role in caring for the oppressed and offer victims and survivors a safe haven of spiritual comfort.

COERCIVE CONTROL—A strategic pattern of ongoing fear tactics intended to pervade all areas of the victim's life to dominate, create compliance and dependency, reduce the ability to act freely, erode the victim's sense of self, and exploit the victim or situation for personal gain. Coercive control leads to entrapment that diminishes the freedom and autonomy of victims. Faith leaders should understand that it is the desire for control that leads to abusive behavior and that patterns of coercive control exist in many abusive relationships. The attitudes behind coercive control are difficult to change and require many years of intentional effort toward correction and rehabilitation.

COLLUDING WITH THE ABUSER—This happens when others take the side of the abuser against the victim. Unfortunately, some abusers will attempt to collude with church leadership against their victims to control the outcome of counseling, small groups, and even church membership. Abusers may use charm and charisma to influence church leadership and congregants into believing their side of the story and shunning the victim. In cases like this, victims generally leave the church for their own well-being. In some cases, churches have preferred to support the abuser and have forced victims out of the church for various reasons. Our holy Scriptures are clear that God's heart is for those who have been oppressed. Faith leaders can respond by taking a careful inventory of situations of abuse, based on the recommendations in this guide.

CONSENT—Permission or agreement for something to happen. Consent is generally freely given within the respectful boundaries of healthy relationships, but toxic relationships disregard it. One area of concern is when victimized spouses are told they must remain sexually available 24/7/365 to keep the husband from having an affair. Availability without consent erodes autonomy and can lead to rape in marriage. No amount of sexual availability on the part of one spouse will cure any part of the other. Using porn and having affairs is never the fault of the victim in the relationship, but rather a conscious choice on the part of the abuser. Pastors can help in these situations by defining consent and making sure the concept is part of premarital and marriage counseling. When seeking to hold abusers accountable, keep in mind that couples counseling is not a safe choice in cases of abuse and sexual assault within the marriage.

COORDINATED COMMUNITY RESPONSE—Involves and brings together multiple community partners for a comprehensive, collaborative response to DV through the common goal of preventing and reducing DV and holding perpetrators accountable. Larger cities and communities may already have a similar organization available that churches can be a part of. Consult your nearest DV organization or state DV resources.

COUPLES COUNSELING—A joint counseling session with both spouses, often designed to reduce or repair conflict in marriage. Joint counseling assumes that both partners are contributing to the conflict and that both partners are willing to work on resolving the issues and putting effort into self-improvement. Unfortunately, in cases of abuse, it is typical for the abuser to be the one creating all the conflict and the victim to be the only one doing the work. This dynamic makes couples counseling contraindicated in cases where abuse exists. Additionally, the person with more power in the relationship will tend to dominate the joint counseling session and may later punish the victim for daring to reveal any portion of their intimate relationship that the perpetrator wants to keep concealed. Clergy, unless trained as professional counselors, should not attempt to engage in couples counseling when abuse is present, but should instead refer cases of abuse to professional individual counselors, or refer the victim to a family violence shelter.

CRAZY MAKING—An atmosphere of confusion created by abusers in which victims begin to doubt their own judgments and perceptions. Abusers change reality, create altered histories, and engage in chaotic emotional manipulation. Abusers are masters of creating confusion in both their victims and others, to take the focus off themselves as perpetrators. Victims subjected to this verbal and emotional tactic may appear to be confused and unsure of themselves. Faith leaders can help by understanding the nature of abuse, by believing victims, and by holding perpetrators accountable for their doublespeak and double standards of conduct. Crazy making is like gaslighting.

CYCLE OF ABUSE—The phases of abusive behavior as described by Lenore Walker: building tension, explosive incident, and honeymoon. Abuse advocates may use this description to explain the repetitious cycle that abuse seems to follow. The tension will build, causing the victim to fear and be cautious. At some point, an explosive incident will occur. The explosive behavior may be physical or could be other forms of abuse, and during this phase, victims may leave to seek safety elsewhere due to the escalation. In the honeymoon stage, the perpetrator may apologize, provide professions of love, give gifts, and use memories of better times to manipulate the victim into staying or coming back to the relationship. Then there is relative calm until the tension starts to build again. Some victims report rapid cycles, and others report slower cycles, but there does tend to be a pattern. It is important to note that explosive incidents do tend to get increasingly worse over time and to understand that victims cannot necessarily predict the patterns of violence. By being aware of the repetitive nature of abuse, faith leaders can better understand what victims and survivors tell them about what they experience, and what is likely to happen again and even grow in intensity. Some advocates have moved away from this language for the reasons given in the corresponding chapter.

DARVO—An acronym that stands for Deny, Attack, and Reverse Victim/Offender, coined by Jennifer Freyd in 1997. It involves the perpetrator denying the abusive behavior, attacking whoever is pointing out the abusive behavior, and then reversing the roles of victim and offender by claiming to be the victim in the situation. It is an attempt to label the actual victim as the offender. This toxic tactic involves denial, minimizing, blame shifting, gaslighting, and projection. The perpetrator can be persuasive enough that the victim begins to doubt recall of the events, and that bystanders join the cause of the perpetrator rather than the victim. A classic example of this behavior would be an abuser telling the pastor that the whole problem was actually his spouse's fault, that he never caused any harm, that she started it, and that he is worried about her spiritual well-being and mental health. Keep in mind that despite the use of this example, men can be victims, and that abuse also exists in same-sex relationships.

Dating violence—Any form of abuse that happens within the dating relationship. It can be an issue for youth, college students, and young adults but may be a concern for older adults as well. Church leadership, and especially youth leaders, ought to offer discussions about healthy relationships, boundaries, consent, and the nature of toxic relationships to help keep congregants safe from perpetrators of abuse in the context of dating relationships. Having these discussions does not increase sexual behavior but rather increases safety and reduces sexual assault.

Domestic homicide—The killing of a victim by an intimate partner. Women are more likely to be killed by a partner or former partner than by anyone else, and most of those killings happen at home. By being aware of this, churches can encourage victims to connect with the local family violence shelter or the family violence department of local law enforcement when they feel their lives are in danger. You can find resources for risk assessment and stalking in appendix A.

ALPHABETICAL GLOSSARY OF DOMESTIC VIOLENCE TERMS

DOMESTIC VIOLENCE SERVICE PROVIDER OR SHELTER—A nonprofit agency generally funded by local, state, and federal grants and generous donors to provide confidential services at no cost to victims and survivors of abuse. Services often include hotlines, counseling, short-term shelter stays, safety planning, legal advocacy, rural outreach, and resource referrals to other local entities including job training, education, financial planning, life skills enhancement, and support groups. Additionally, shelters often provide prevention and community awareness events, and training about DV, teen dating violence, and child abuse. Church leadership should be aware of the nearest shelter and make a point to reach out to the director for information about the services offered, ideally before there is a need to refer a congregant to the shelter.

DOORMAT THEOLOGY—Religious platitudes that encourage victims to stay in abuse. These harmful ideals involve telling the victim to stay, pray, and submit. They use Scripture to require the victim to turn the other cheek, forgive and forget, endure suffering patiently, overcome evil with good, engage in fervent prayer, and be silently submissive in all things. Most victims are already engaging in these activities, even without being told to do so, although messages such as these are common in some faith communities. Doormat theology does not end the abuse. In some cases, the more the victim submits, the more violent the abuse becomes. Church teaching along these lines coupled with a lack of condemnation from the church regarding the abusive behavior essentially provides permission for the abuse to continue. Clergy and other faith leaders should seek education and awareness regarding DV to eliminate dangerous teaching that may put victims at risk of further harm. If it comes to a pastor's attention that doormat theology is used, care can be taken to correct these ideas and provide safe and supportive spaces for those healing from abuse. It is important to remember that the Bible also states the need to resist evil and flee from it, to have nothing to do with the fruitless deeds of darkness. Those who do evil must turn from it and pursue peace.

ALPHABETICAL GLOSSARY OF DOMESTIC VIOLENCE TERMS

Double standard—The abuser minimizes personal involvement and maximizes beliefs about any wrongs the victim may have committed. It can also mean that the perpetrator is free to act in any way desired, but the victim is held to a higher (maybe even unattainable) standard. In other words, even the church may expect the victim or survivor to be perfect while granting the abuser the benefit of the doubt. Or the abuser acts with impunity while the victim is silenced with allegations of gossip. Sadly, the frequency with which this happens in churches is quite high, as reported by victims and survivors themselves. Clergy and other faith leaders can eliminate this mentality by promoting equality between genders and holding everyone to the same standard. Take care that abusers do not blame their victims and evade personal responsibility. Take care not to gaslight victims or utilize doormat theology. Make it clear that teachings on Christian character and the fruit of the Spirit are applicable to all believers equally.

Elder abuse—In cases where it intersects with domestic violence, this encompasses any form of abuse or neglect perpetrated against an older person by an intimate partner or former partner. When older adults experience the overlap of domestic violence and elder abuse, they may be able to receive services from multiple agencies. Also, check with your state's mandated reporting laws to see if this is a matter that must be reported to Adult Protective Services.

Entitlement—An idea possessed by many abusers that they deserve special treatment and privileges. Entitlement causes them to violate boundaries and act as they wish, without remorse. In a Christian environment, the perpetrator may tangle entitlement with spiritual abuse in claiming a biblical right to the spouse's body, finances, property, or time. The church can help by speaking against the concept of special rights and privileges due to gender or status. We are all equal in Christ, neither male nor female, bond nor free, Jew nor Greek. Entitlement has no place in the Christian life of service, stewardship, and humility.

False repentance—False apologies and promises utilized to make the victim, and others, think that change has occurred.

False repentance may happen in cases where the abuser is seeking reconciliation with the victim, or as a way of manipulating clergy, church lay leaders, or the court system. Signs of false repentance include continued bitterness or ill will, lying and deceit, slander, and lack of change in behavior over time. Often abusers can maintain superficial changes in behavior in connection with false repentance for a time, but not indefinitely. Words that indicate remorse do not necessarily mean that a person has made long-lasting behavioral changes. Faith leaders do victims a disservice when they accept words of change at face value, without prolonged observation to see whether a true change has really occurred. Appendix E has a list to assess genuine change over time.

FEAR TACTICS—Manipulative behaviors used to keep the victim under control. Fear tactics can include breaking furniture, punching walls, throwing dinner across the room, incessant yelling, brandishing weapons, injuring pets, or other behaviors designed to instill fear into the victim. The abuser may exhibit rage and anger, but fear tactics can also be covert emotional abuse in the form of threats of harm and intimidation. A perpetrator can instill fear without resorting to violence. Just a look or a phrase from the perpetrator can be enough to raise distress levels in the victim when fear tactics and coercive control are involved. Churches should know that when someone verbalizes being afraid of an intimate partner, this is a warning sign of significant abuse. Refer the victim to a family violence shelter or the family violence department of the police or sheriff's station. If a perpetrator uses fear tactics and threats against clergy or other members of the congregation, consider which authorities may need to be involved to address the issue.

FLYING MONKEYS—This unusual term references the monkeys who did the bidding of the Wicked Witch in *The Wizard of Oz*. Abusers surround themselves with those who will do their bidding to create havoc on the victim, through grooming, guilting, and lying to the flying monkeys, who may or may not be aware of the abusive dynamics displayed. The flying monkeys then take up the cause of the perpetrator and participate in harmful behaviors. By not condemning the abuse, they are in fact participating in it. If enough flying monkeys get involved, it creates something of a mob of attackers all working against the victim. Another way to describe this is "abuse by proxy" because the abuser is using a third party to generate the damage. Victims and survivors are particularly devastated when the flying monkey is a child, parent, relative, friend, or close colleague. Due to the prior close relationship, the victim can feel deeply betrayed and the grief involved can be intense. Signs of betrayal within a congregation may be visible when the abuser appears to be recruiting allies and spreading gossip against the victim. When this happens, victims lose their sense of security within the church community, and it becomes safer for them to leave the church than to stay. Those who leave the church to protect themselves should not be faulted for doing so. Congregational leadership needs to be aware of such tactics, denounce their use, and protect the victim(s) from such harmful actions.

FORGIVENESS—A decision on the part of the victim to release the betrayal, anger, and hurt caused by the abuse. It is unwise and harmful to force forgiveness or require it within a certain time period. It is a long and complex process and only the victim should dictate the timeline. Forgiveness does not equal forgetting, nor require reconciliation. It does not give the abuser a free pass for the abuse to continue. A victim can forgive, and yet still name and acknowledge the damage. Requiring forgiveness despite no evidence of genuine repentance further harms victims and survivors of DV.

FUTURE FAKING—A made-up future filled with glowing details of fabulous times. It may include grandiose plans for the exact future the victim has claimed to desire. It makes things look so good that the victim is coerced into agreeing to things now in order to secure the projected perfect future. For example, the victim agrees to get engaged or married quickly, moves cross-country, or gives up friends and family, based on plans for a fake future that will never exist. The victim honestly believes that everything is real and is swept up in the excitement, but it never materializes the way the victim believes that it will. This is often combined with other abusive and red-flag tactics like love bombing, grooming, isolation, coercive control, and/or gaslighting.

GASLIGHTING—Taken from the 1940 movie *Gaslight*, this term refers to the act of making a person doubt their own memory or perceptions, thus feeling they are going crazy. It is the intentional misrepresentation of words, items, and events used to emotionally manipulate another person. Examples include pretending like it never happened, creating a false narrative, distorting facts, blaming the victim, and causing a person to doubt memories. To create further devastation, the abuser might claim the victim is upset, overreacting, confused, defensive, or lying. Engaging in gaslighting does not display the nature of godly behavior. Churches can speak against destructive and harmful behavior that tears people down while emphasizing scriptural concepts such as kindness, goodness, truthfulness, and pure speech that edifies those who hear it.

GENDER ROLE EXPECTATIONS—There is a long history of protecting and enforcing gender roles within some faith communities. If gender roles are rigidly enforced, generally male dominance and female submission are expected. Male abusers often use gender role language in connection with spiritual abuse to maintain the imbalance of power in a relationship by requiring absolute submission. In these cases, women may not be allowed to work outside the home, attend college, chose their own attire, have financial independence, or freely visit friends and family. Female abusers may ridicule sensitivity, empathy, or the considerate feelings of a spouse. The Bible exhibits many examples contrary to strict gender roles. Compassionate males and strong female leaders are both featured in Scripture. Churches can help by encouraging congregants to all live in harmony according to the fruit of the Spirit, engage in servant leadership, and apply the Golden Rule in marriage.

GRAY DIVORCE—Divorce involving individuals over age fifty. Women who seek divorce in their later years often name abuse and their spouse's pornography addiction or affairs as the reasons they do so. Years of blame, shame, use, and abuse will have taken their toll. These abused women may stay until the children are older before taking this step. Instead of assuming they are throwing away years of a good marriage, seek to understand the depth of any pain behind such a decision. Was there abuse? Can you refer them for professional counseling? How can the church help? Offer compassion and understanding, while also providing resources and support as needed. Abuse in elderly couples may require the use of Adult Protective Services.

GRAY ROCK—A response mechanism that victims of abuse can use to decrease the intensity of inflammatory conversation with the abuser. This is a method coined in 2012 by a mental health blogger known as Skylar, who basically advocated for becoming as "boring as a rock" in communication after exiting high-conflict relationships. Abusers who crave consistent drama often use manipulative, dramatic tactics to induce a heated response from the victim or survivor. The gray rock technique includes short, simple, bland, disengaged answers that stick to the facts and leave emotion out of the response. The de-escalated response is about as interesting as a gray rock, and thus the term. Victims can use the gray rock technique when going no contact isn't an option. Yellow rock is a version of this that some survivors choose to use when children or the family court system make additional communication more necessary.

GREEN FLAGS—Characteristics of healthy relationships with good boundaries and autonomy for both partners. Often survivors fear getting into a new relationship due to previous harm in abusive relationships. Green flags are the qualities to look for. Green flag behaviors are based on equality, mutual respect, consent, trust, kindness, open dialogue, safety, support, and freedom to disagree. Churches can promote healthy relationships in congregants by talking about these qualities, which are reflective of a mature Christian life. Green flags can also be part of the healthy versus toxic relationship discussion that should occur within all age groups at the church.

ALPHABETICAL GLOSSARY OF DOMESTIC VIOLENCE TERMS

GROOMING—A predatory tool used by abusers to gain access to a potential victim, or to gain allies to minimize detection and prosecution. It includes targeting, befriending, and establishing an emotional connection as a means of lowering inhibitions for the purpose of manipulating, exploiting, or violating the individual. Grooming may involve years of deception and include secret communication, gifts, or inappropriate touch. The person doing the grooming will pretend to make the victim feel loved and attempt to fill an emotional need. As the grooming progresses, the abuser will test boundaries and may use intimidation and threats to keep the victim from speaking out or trying to get away. Abusers use grooming tactics online or in dating apps, in child sexual assault, human trafficking, clergy sexual assault, and in abusive relationships. Abusers will also groom bystanders or flying monkeys to display prejudice against the victim. By being aware of the predatory but secretive nature of grooming, faith leaders can put safeguards and boundaries in place to protect congregants. Many churches are putting child protection policies in place, but fewer have protections against clergy sexual assault, and even fewer have plans for helping victims caught in abusive relationships. Partnering with local entities to train church staff and lay leaders will help educate congregations and provide awareness about the dangers of predatory behavior.

GUILT—Victims often internalize guilt about the abuse, guilt about staying in the abuse, or even guilt about leaving the abuse. They may think they did something to cause the abuse because that is what their abusers tell them. They may feel guilty for not being able to stop the abuse or for bringing children into an abusive marriage. A victim may stay in an abusive relationship due to guilt or shame about family reputation. Victims are often guilted by the abuser, and sometimes by their church. If anyone in authority has instructed the victim to stay, pray, forgive, and submit, it likely added to the feelings of guilt. Faith leaders can help victims and survivors of abuse know that it was not their fault and help them obtain freedom from feelings of false guilt. A referral for professional counseling may be necessary.

ALPHABETICAL GLOSSARY OF DOMESTIC VIOLENCE TERMS

HEALTHY RELATIONSHIPS—Healthy relationships are built on a foundation of respect, equality, trust, and honest communication. They are interdependent and show mutual support, and each party retains an identity as a unique individual. In a balanced relationship, neither person maintains strict control and neither person is fully submissive. Behavior is never threatening. In healthy marriages, both individuals take personal responsibility and work on productive communication. Churches can promote healthy relationships by having age-appropriate conversations about healthy versus toxic relationships at all age levels and groups within the church. Label toxic behavior appropriately and describe what it looks like. Discuss healthy boundaries and their importance in relationships. Have conversations about consent. Healthy relationships provide a beautiful picture of how Christ loves and cares for us.

HOOVERING—The term's origin is based on the Hoover vacuum. It refers to the emotional abuse and manipulation that an abuser uses to "suck" the victim back into the relationship. It may include grandiose gestures and love bombing to persuade the victim not to leave, or to return to the relationship. It might include "accidental" contact, reminiscent messages, or promises of better times. After previously treating the victim quite poorly, Hoovering is a confusing phase of sudden attention and new promises. Hoovering can also be used to retain individuals who are allies and flying monkeys.

HOPE—Despite the trauma and often despite lack of support, victims desire to anticipate a future without violence. While still in a destructive marriage, the individual may hope for a changed spouse or a healed marriage. After escaping abuse there can be considerable challenges due to post-separation abuse and court hearings that affect the ability to maintain hope. Victims and survivors need to feel that hope is still alive. They need to see their faith leaders as a resource and their church as a place of safety. When clergy and fellow congregants believe in survivors and support them, it provides hope and healing after the trauma of abuse.

INTERSECTIONALITY—In the context of abuse, this is the overlap of abuse with other vulnerabilities. It considers how someone's various life circumstances might contribute to being oppressed in a relationship. Those with disabilities, women of color, immigrants, refugees, and the LGBTQ+ community experience intimate partner violence, and yet these individuals may struggle to have equal access to assistance due to social bias. Churches can assist by understanding the complexity of barriers to services, and by believing victims when they describe how their abuse is complicated by stigma, bias, prejudice, racism, or other factors. As advocates and allies, we do not want to tell others what they are feeling as that would be parallel to gaslighting. Rather we should accept and believe their experiences as described, even if we do not understand the nuances of the situation.

ISOLATION—A tactic of control used by the abuser to separate the victim from the support of family, friends, school, work, church, or another source of assistance. Abusers use isolation to carry out the abuse in secret. Isolation used with other forms of abuse can eliminate outside influence and make the victim more dependent. Without other voices of reason, the victim doesn't have anyone to help identify destructive behaviors. Physical isolation may include requiring the victim to stay at home and not work or attend school, uprooting the family and moving far away, or controlling whom the victim can visit or talk to. Spiritual isolation might look like not allowing church attendance or requiring attendance only at certain places of worship. Be alert to signs of isolation as a tactic of abuse. Families who land in your congregation without family or support systems, after moving frequently, may be subject to isolation. A carefully timed check-in with the suspected victim can lead to more information, but be careful to not put the suspected victim at further risk of harm.

JEST—The abuser may at times say things in jest or use humor to disguise unkind, derogatory, and manipulative words. As a part of multiple patterns of toxic behavior, this can be a sign of verbal and/or emotional abuse. Jesting is an especially cruel form of abusive behavior because others outside the relationship will tend to side with the abuser, thinking the victim is just too sensitive or lacking a sense of humor. Churches can help encourage healthy behavior by promoting pure and gracious speech that is edifying to those who hear it. Additionally, set aside potentially harmful illustrations in conversations or sermons designed to produce a laugh but that may be harmful to survivors of abuse.

LETHALITY—Certain behaviors and situations that pose a greater risk of lethal harm to the victim. Abusers may use volatile or depressive behavior combined with threats to kill the victim, children, family, pets, or self. The availability of weapons, especially firearms, raises the risk of lethality significantly. Prior incidents of strangulation drastically increase the risk of homicide. Other risk factors include substance use, unemployment, and stalking. Faith leaders must be aware of the behaviors most likely to cause serious injury or death to protect the vulnerable in their congregations. Knowledge of any alarming behaviors indicates a need for safety planning. It is best to refer those in danger to a family violence shelter or law enforcement family violence units.

LETHALITY ASSESSMENT—An assessment tool to help identify risk or the likelihood of the perpetrator causing severe injury. Law enforcement personnel and family violence shelters use these assessments in their efforts to reduce family violence homicides. The presence of a weapon, particularly firearms, and a history of strangulation in the relationship are high indicators of future homicide.

LOVE BOMBING—The act of influencing another person through gift-giving, lavish praise, and intense overwhelming attention. It can involve promises of a perfect life and declarations of love earlier in the relationship than would generally be expected. It is a form of strategic emotional abuse used to lower one's guard. Quick engagements and hasty marriages can be a result of love bombing. The relationship may seem too good to be true. Any doubt, hesitation, or boundaries on the part of the victim may elicit jealous, possessive behavior in return, often followed by additional love bombing to keep the victim trapped in the relationship. Faith leaders who are aware of this tactic of abuse can help the intended victim by discussing the reality of the relationship. However, those caught up in the love-bombing stage may not be able to see the danger of the situation. Youth, college, and young adult pastors and lay leaders who work with these age groups should be aware of love bombing in dating relationships and speak about toxic behavior patterns before congregants end up in dangerous relationships.

MARGINALIZE—Treating someone as insignificant, pushing them to the margins, and keeping them unimportant and powerless. In the context of abuse, it might be related to barriers to services for minorities or those with disabilities. Faith communities participate in marginalizing victims when they don't listen well or believe the victim, when they collude with the abuser, when they slander survivors, or when they place focus on preserving the marriage rather than condemning the abuse. Being aware of this reduces the likelihood of additional harm.

MINIMIZING THE ABUSE—A tactic of emotional abuse used to dismiss or reduce the severity or urgency of the abusive behavior. Minimizing is a way of saying that someone's words, experiences, or feelings don't matter. Churches engage in minimizing the abuse when they encourage the victim to forgive and forget, claim the abuse wasn't that bad, or blame the victim for causing the abuse. Instead, churches can support victims by believing them, helping with safety planning, and referring them to additional sources of assistance.

MIRRORING—In the context of abuse, the abuser creates a reflection that looks just like the victim and pretends to be just what the victim desires in the relationship. There is a supposed love for the same food, music, activities, vacation spots, pets, passions, desires in life, etc. Mirroring creates an illusion of intimacy that doesn't really exist. Combined and alternated with other forms of verbal or emotional abuse, mirroring is one of many relational red flags. The church can provide caution to congregants by talking about healthy and toxic relationships.

MISOGYNY—The contempt for and devaluing of women. An idea that women cannot have equal power in relationships, society, or the church. It may assert that a husband or father mediates between a female and God. In a faith-based context, it is a view that God created women to be in subjection to men, rather than seeing hierarchy in relationships as a result of the fall in the garden of Eden. The church can work against misogyny by affirming that God created women equal in God's image, by reminding congregants that all believers have equal access directly to God without the need for a mediator, by speaking of equality in healthy relationships, and by placing women in positions of leadership within the church. Men need to hear from their faith leaders that they are to engage the same love, care, and concern for their wives that Christ bestows on the church.

MOOD SWINGS—From feigning sweetness to displaying rage, this is also known as Jekyll and Hyde behavior. Mood swings can be sudden and intense changes in behavior with little to no provocation. Often the abuser pretends to be charming in public but is toxic behind closed doors at home where there are no observers to see the abusive behavior. Faith leaders can ascertain the truth about someone's behavior by asking the victim what the abuser is like at home when no one is watching. It might be hard to believe that the abuser is vicious and vindictive at home if they display only good behavior at church, but it happens frequently. The best response is to believe victims and validate their experiences.

MUTUAL ABUSE—Describes a relationship where both partners are abusive and use toxic behaviors against each other. There may be rare instances of this happening, but in most cases, the truth points to one aggressor and one who is engaging in self-defense. There are not always two truthful sides to every story, and it is not wise or fair to automatically place mutual blame on both parties in an abusive relationship. The trauma of abuse can cause the victim to be confused and disorientated. An abuser has probably subjected the victim to toxicity for years, which can create unhealthy, and even reactionary, coping mechanisms on the part of the victim. If it looks like both parties have used violence, consider which partner holds control in the relationship and if one was acting in self-defense. Keep in mind that some abusers will bait the victim to get a response, and then use that response to blame the victim. This does not display love and godly character, but rather self-serving behavior on the part of the perpetrator.

NARCISSISTIC PERSONALITY DISORDER (NPD)—A diagnosable personality disorder demonstrated by a sense of entitlement, inflated sense of self and personal accomplishments, need for attention and praise, an expectation of special treatment, delusions of grandeur, history of exploiting others, a lack of empathy, and negative reactions to boundaries and criticism. Those with NPD usually have a history of failed relationships for which they blame their partner for the problems. Men are more likely to have NPD than women and are more likely to be aggressive and drawn to positions of power. A mental health professional must screen the individuals before providing a diagnosis. Unfortunately, few narcissistic abusers choose to admit a problem and seek treatment, which means that many go undiagnosed. Many abusers do have narcissistic traits, but it is wise to use caution in diagnosing someone without professional training and licensure.

NO CONTACT—A survival technique used by victims of abuse in an attempt to reclaim control over their own lives. No contact is not the same thing as the silent treatment. Abusers will use silent treatment against their victims out of anger or spite. In contrast, no contact is a way of using boundaries to protect oneself against continued harm from the one who has repeatedly created injuries. In cases where minor-aged children are involved, a no contact boundary might be impossible, but in these cases, the victim can use the gray rock or yellow rock method to create boundaries for safety while still engaging in minimal interaction. At times, courts establish no contact orders as a way of protecting victims and survivors from those who perpetrate harm against them. Violations of court-ordered no contact orders can lead to criminal charges.

PLAYING THE VICTIM—A manipulative tactic of the abuser to feign innocence or helplessness. It is a way to groom others by seeking pity from those who are empathetic to other people's distress. The problem here is that any supposed suffering in these cases is what the abuser fakes and uses to hook the empathetic onlooker. It often includes blaming problems on other people or other issues to avoid responsibility. The abuser may even resort to self-injury to get sympathy or to accuse the victim of being abusive as in cases of DARVO. The best response is to be alert to victim-like behavior in connection with additional behavioral red flags and other signs of DV.

POST-SEPARATION ABUSE—Any form of abuse that continues after the separation or divorce. It is not enough that these victims endured abuse throughout the marriage. Out of spite or revenge or a continued desire for control, perpetrators will engage in continued stalking and harassment. They may start a smear campaign to turn friends and family against the victim. If there are children in the relationship, the abuser will use the children as pawns to hurt a former spouse. These abusers manipulate the court systems by bringing continuous and expensive litigation, even to the point of bankrupting a former spouse. They may refuse to pay child support or to reimburse for their portion of children's expenses. They may seek to separate a survivor from any systems of support. Such behavior clearly shows ungodly attitudes and actions, and pastoral staff or leadership must seek to protect the victim and children from continued harm with the use of safety planning and other measures of assistance. If strangulation or weapons are involved, it would be wise to put the victim in contact with the police for a lethality assessment.

POWER AND CONTROL—Abusers use a variety of abusive behaviors to gain and maintain control over the victim and exploit vulnerabilities. Christian relationships should never be dominated by power and control but should rather display fairness, equality, and respect. Churches can help by including discussions of power and control in age-appropriate discussions of relationships. Power and control wheels are available to assist in awareness and education on this topic. Check appendix A for these helpful tools.

PROJECTION—In cases of abuse, this is attributing one's own negative attributes to another. It is a tactic used to discredit the victim by projecting the abuser's own negative behavior, emotions, or character traits onto the victim. It is a form of denial and blame shifting and displays a lack of accountability. Some experts say that projection by the abuser is an admission of all the wrongs committed against the victim. For example, an abuser may blame the victim for having an affair, when in fact the abuser has been having an affair all along. Clergy can take inventory of who holds the most power in the relationship and consider the accusations made rather than automatically believing the more vocal or persuasive spouse. It should also be noted that projection can be reversed and used the other way as well. Faith leaders may project goodness onto the perpetrators because they would never behave in this manner. Victims may project their desire to heal a toxic marriage onto the perpetrator believing that the perpetrator will desire the same goal. Whether the ideas being projected originate from the belief that the other party is either evil or good, the projection will distort the relationship and cloud judgment. Clear, honest communication is always the best policy.

RAPE CULTURE—Allows men to keep power without requiring accountability. It blames women for what they were wearing, where they were going, or what they were doing. Rape culture reinforces patterns of dominance against women and silences them, including the use of pornography and dehumanizing depictions of violence against women. Rape culture normalizes sexual assault, "locker-room talk," and stereotypes. Misogyny allows rape culture and sexual assault to flourish. Faith communities reinforce rape culture when they blame women and put the responsibility for purity on them, rather than holding men accountable for toxic behavior. In youth groups, this looks like emphasizing how girls should dress rather than requiring that boys conduct themselves appropriately. Rape culture is damaging to our churches and society and must end.

RAPE IN MARRIAGE—Rape is the use of force or coercion to require sexual acts. Rape can, and does, happen in marriage, and is a form of intimate partner violence. Marriage does not grant full and complete access to the spouse's body. Some marriage advice seems to encourage a husband's unrestricted access to a wife's body to cure marriage difficulties. However, requiring a spouse to be a sexual object will not cure abuse and will only make things worse. Reject such notions by understanding the boundaries of healthy relationships, including respect between partners in the bedroom. Marital rape is a crime in all fifty states.

RECONCILIATION—It is unwise and unfeeling to encourage or force victims of abuse to reconcile. The idea behind forced reconciliation in some faith communities is that all marriages are salvageable, and that abuse is not an acceptable reason to separate or divorce. However, forcing a victim to stay, or return to the abuse, is dangerous. False repentance is possible. True change is difficult and takes years, and not all perpetrators are willing to do the hard work that reconciliation requires. In cases where the spouse perpetrating violence claims to want to change, the church can require that the perpetrator attend batterer's intervention courses and support the use of civil protective orders. If a victim of abuse chooses to attempt reconciliation, counseling, safety planning, risk assessment, and the provision of a support system will be necessary. The victim will need to be assured that if the abuse escalates, there is no obligation to remain in a dangerous home.

RED FLAGS—Dangerous or unhealthy characteristics displayed by someone with abusive tendencies. Red flags include (but are not limited to) grooming, jealousy, anger, possessiveness, ridicule, criticism, lies, manipulation, fear tactics, isolation, control, double standards, blame, demanding respect, power imbalance, stalking, and past abusive behavior. Disregarding the law, fascination with weapons, high pressure, ignoring boundaries, lack of respect, substance misuse, and neglect can all be red flags as well. Often the red flags are subtle at first and individuals dismiss them as less serious than they really are. It is important that red flags are not ignored in an individual or in a relationship as they are a sign of bigger problems ahead. Churches should include red flags as part of the discussion of healthy and toxic relationships, discussions of dating and marriage, and premarital counseling.

Resilience—In this context, it is the ability to adapt, recover, grow, and thrive after DV. Victims become survivors after they leave the abuse and start to heal. Each victim possesses the strength to escape the abuse, to create a new life free of physical and emotional violence, and often to help children recover from witnessing abuse. Children who have witnessed abuse or experienced child abuse often need support to recover. Trauma-informed professional counseling may be part of the recovery strategy. Although each victim possesses strength and a level of resilience, some find it difficult to access. One of the best ways to increase resilience is the presence of support from those who understand the nature of abuse and are willing to do the work of eliminating it. Churches can aid in resilience by believing the victim, offering emotional and social support, providing tangible assistance, and making sure the church is a safe, abuse-free environment. Additionally, conversations about faith and spirituality can be helpful to survivors wishing to include this in their healing journey. Churches should seek awareness and education about DV as one way to aid the resilience of those who have experienced it.

Revenge porn—Also known as nonconsensual distribution of intimate images. A tool of manipulation to keep the victim within the control of the abuser. This heinous tactic of abuse is frequent in dating relationships but can also happen in marriage, and often intersects with other forms of verbal and emotional abuse, including post-separation abuse. There can be a considerable amount of shame for the victim if the abuser threatens to, or does, spread these around to those in their acquaintance. Such behavior has no place in a Christian relationship.

ALPHABETICAL GLOSSARY OF DOMESTIC VIOLENCE TERMS

SAFETY PLANNING—An emergency plan ideally made before there is a need for it. It can help lower risk and provide guidance when a DV situation gets out of control. Safety planning can vary by individual and situation but should include ways to increase safety at home, work, school, and with phones and media. Safety planning is necessary if the victim intends to separate from the abuser and believes there to be a risk of personal or property injury. Those experiencing abuse should keep the safety plan in a secure location. Family violence shelters generally offer free safety planning for their clients. Pastors can use safety planning with congregants who need to plan for future safety. This information can be found in appendix A.

SECRETS—Some secrets are harmful. Secrets accompanied by a threat to keep silent need to be shared. Abuse thrives in secrecy, and much abuse goes undetected and unreported because of this. These are important conversations to have with everyone, but especially with children and youth, along with discussions of boundaries and consent. Child abuse, clergy sexual assault, sexual abuse, rape, and revenge porn are crimes that create shame and guilt. By understanding the criminal nature of some abuse, and the detrimental nature of all abuse, churches can support victims and be advocates against abuse of all kinds. It can also be helpful to differentiate secrets from surprises. A surprise refers to something kept quiet for a short time and then revealed, often with celebration.

SHAME—When the victim feels unworthy, unloved, and worthless. The victim may feel shame for getting into a toxic relationship, or for staying in it. The victim may feel shame over sexual assault. Shame can lead to despair and self-loathing. Family, friends, and the faith community might (consciously or unconsciously) heap additional shame on the victim. The church can help by referring the victim to a licensed counselor trained in dealing with DV and trauma. The church can also assure the victim of each person's worth and identity in Christ, and the ability to leave shame behind when healing after abuse.

SMEAR CAMPAIGN—An intentional attempt to damage and destroy the victim's life and reputation. A smear campaign may involve lies, misleading statements, and deception to discredit the victim among their friends and in their faith community. An abuser may use a smear campaign with the couple's children to slander the other parent. The church can help by not engaging in such conversation and by supporting the victim. It is also helpful to understand that it is hard to reason with abusers. Attempts by clergy to end the smear campaign, possibly as a form of church discipline, may be met with resistance. Any resistance to attempts for accountability and changed behavior are indicative of a person who is not displaying repentance.

STALKING—Stalking occurs when the perpetrator monitors activities, spies on, and/or chooses to follow, harass, and engage in repeated unwanted attention or spiteful communication. It may include unwanted gifts, threats, communication, spyware, or GPS locators and tracking systems. It can include using home security systems against the victim. Stalking behavior creates a credible threat for the victim, causing emotional distress and fears for safety. Stalking is a crime. Unfortunately, the media often portrays one person heavily pursuing another early in a relationship as romantic or endearing. Such portrayals are misleading because this is not always the case. When the pursuit, the surprise visits, the constant texting, or the unexpected gifts are about power and control, they can signal toxic and dangerous behavior. If you are aware of stalking behavior, engage in conversations about red flags and safety planning. Have conversations with youth and young adults about the inappropriateness of stalking behavior. If needed, put the victim in touch with a family violence shelter or the police for information on how to report the crime.

STRANGULATION—If a victim of abuse reports strangulation or choking, know that you are dealing with a crime. Strangulation is a felony assault and attempted homicide. It is possible to experience strangulation and not have visible marks. Medical imaging studies show that much of the damage is internal and unseen.

Strangulation is a lethal form of abuse, and prior history of strangulation in the relationship increases the risk of homicide by 750 percent. Victims of strangulation lose consciousness within six seconds and death occurs in one to three minutes. Partners who are willing to strangle their victims are more likely to go to greater lengths to injure and kill. Churches can help by getting victims connected to the local family violence shelter, the family violence unit at a police department, or a medical center. Remember that the victim should always be the one to make the decision about involving others. There may be extenuating circumstances in the relationship that put the victim in greater danger. See appendix A for additional resources.

TOXIC RELATIONSHIPS—A relationship characterized by jealousy, resentment, anger, guilt, blame, shame, humiliation, coercive control, disrespect, lack of accountability, hostility, lack of trust, inequality, or any form of abuse. Toxic relationships display red flags. They often happen quickly, and one person may have to give up everything for the other. These relationships exhibit struggles that peaceful dialogue cannot resolve. When a person realizes that toxic behavior exists and decides to leave the relationship, that person should engage in safety planning due to possible risks and dangers. A church can help by talking about healthy and toxic relationships, calling out abusive behaviors and attitudes, promoting equality between genders, and holding people accountable. Although the purpose of this book is to discuss intimate partner relationships, know that toxicity can exist in friendships, families, work environments, and other relationships including faith communities. It is important to guard against all types of toxicity and strive to promote healthy relationships.

TRAUMA—A normal response to abuse. Victims have had their perceived safety shattered, which creates trauma and devastation in their lives. Abuse affects both physical and mental health, and symptoms are likely to persist without intervention. The church can assist by referring victims to a trauma-informed therapist. Often family violence shelters will provide no-cost counseling for victims and survivors. Churches should engage in trauma-informed training events to best provide supportive services to those who need them because there are many reasons that congregants may experience trauma.

TRAUMA BOND—Abusive relationships don't start with abusive acts. There are the typical beginnings of attraction and romance that create an emotional bond. The emotional bond is often well established when the abuser begins to test the boundaries of the relationship. Emotional turmoil is created as the abuser alternates abusive explosions with love bombing and good times. By the time a victim begins to wonder about the toxicity of the relationship, the emotional bond will already be in place. Victims may rationalize or dismiss what seem like insignificant problems in the beginning because they want the relationship to continue. Some victims will defend the abuser's behavior and isolate themselves from those who display concern. Faith leaders who suspect that a congregant may have trauma bonds can offer to refer the victim to a therapist trained to care for these situations or a family violence shelter. Education and awareness are key to overcoming the bond in a toxic relationship. Churches can also create a safe space, present resources, provide support, and encourage the victim to share freely while attempting to heal.

TRAUMA-INFORMED CARE—Refers to specific way of responding to trauma that considers the complexity of the experience, and how trauma affects the lives of those who experience it. It includes considering safety, victim choice, collaboration with service providers, cultural sensitivity, intersectionality, support, and empowerment. It seeks to give agency to survivors and respond to them in ways that do not re-traumatize them.

TRIANGULATION—An emotionally abusive tactic used to turn others against the victim through manipulative interactions. It can involve bringing another person or group into the interaction to abuse the victim. It might be an attempt to make the victim angry or jealous, by having affairs or comparing the victim to others regarding appearance, personality, abilities, or education. The abuser may try to get clergy and other professionals (doctors, counselors, court officials, etc.) to take their side against the victim. Triangulation can include slander and manufactured allegations to portray the victim in a negative light. The church can intervene by understanding this abusive technique and being willing to stand against such behavior.

TRIGGER—A word, conversation, image, action, touch, smell, sound, etc. that brings a memory of the DV back to the surface and transports the person back to the moment of the trauma. Triggers can be caused by any of the senses. They take a survivor back to recollections of the abuse, cause flashbacks, create anxiety or a panic attack, and bring up feelings of danger. They can cause a person to become ill, tearful, fearful, defensive, or withdrawn. There is no way for you to know exactly what triggers each individual survivor, but when you do know, please act with caution. If you encounter a survivor who has been triggered, show empathy, and recognize that this is part of what survivors learn to deal with after leaving abuse, but that it takes time to heal the myriad of trauma symptoms. Counseling will help with trigger management, which is one reason that trauma-informed professional therapy is vital for recovery after abuse. Triggers may also be known as *activating content* in some literature.

VICTIM BLAMING—The response of an individual or group to blame the victim rather than blaming the one who has engaged in harmful behavior. This includes asking victims what they could have done to keep the abuse from happening. It would include blaming one spouse for the other's pornography addiction. Another example would be blaming the wife for not being submissive enough, rather than the husband for yelling and screaming at her. Alternatively, it could mean blaming the husband for not keeping his home in order. In the context of dating violence, it would include blaming sexual assault victims by asking what they were wearing, if they were drinking, or where they were going. The best approach for faith leaders is to be conscious of such behavior and to take care that conversation and actions are free of victim blame.

VICTIM-CENTERED APPROACH—A professional standard for trauma-informed care that centers on understanding and responding to the victim's experiences in a way that encompasses dignity and respect. It compassionately focuses on their well-being, safety, and needs. It centers victim voices while encouraging their agency and self-determination in the process of healing. It includes cultural sensitivity and considers intersectionality when working with minority populations. Faith communities should seek to engage in this approach when working with victims and survivors of abuse. Sometimes the automatic reaction is to protect the perpetrator and question or blame the victim over what caused the abusive behavior, but that causes further harm. Start by listening, believing, and validating the victim's experiences. Empower survivors to make their own choices. Be there to provide support as needed through the healing process. Engage in trauma training seminars and seek to be a trauma-informed congregation.

WALKING ON EGGSHELLS—How victims describe having to act around an abusive partner. In a volatile environment, the victim feels the need to alter actions and words to not upset the abuser. The unpredictable environment keeps the victim from being free to act in a normal manner and pressures the victim to acquiesce to demands to keep peace in the home. Tension, nonverbal cues, violent outbursts, or erratic behavior keep the victim anxious about what will happen next. If someone ever describes a relationship in this way, it is a warning sign to clergy and other faith leaders that something is amiss in that relationship. A careful conversation may lead to additional clues that would give a better understanding of the relationship, and an opportunity to refer this person to helpful resources.

YELLOW ROCK—A communication method that is a bit more gracious than gray rock and differs due to added courtesies and politeness to appear a bit more friendly. It may be helpful in disputed custody situations where communication goes through the family court system or required communication app, and where no contact or gray rock may not be possible. This method was coined by Tina Swithin, who has highlighted post-separation abuse and court-related divorce issues for victims and survivors of DV. Gray rock and yellow rock are skills that survivors may need to learn, as they don't always come naturally. It helps to limit conversations to texts or email so that there is a paper trail, rather than phone conversations, which can be triggering. Clergy and lay leaders can help by understanding the nature of abuse and the tactics of abusers. Toxic methods of communication are not in accordance with the fruit of the Spirit. It is hard for victims to heal if constantly harassed by post-separation abuse, so reducing friction can increase mental health and overall well-being. Using gray rock or yellow rock techniques can be helpful in decreasing or eliminating hurtful communication.

Appendix A: Resources

DUE TO THE EVER-CHANGING nature of the internet and how resources are cataloged and accessed, please visit the comprehensive list of resources, including topics of clergy-mandated reporting, divorce, domestic violence, the Experience of Harm graphic, finding a local shelter, safety, stalking, strangulation, and more, on this book's website: TakingItSeriously.com

To learn more about the author's domestic violence advocacy and awareness projects, please visit:

HopeRiseThrive.com

@Hope.Rise.Thrive on Facebook and Instagram

HOTLINES

National Child Abuse Hotline
https://www.childhelp.org/
1-800-422-4453

National Dating Abuse Hotline
https://www.loveisrespect.org/
1-866-331-9474

National Domestic Violence Hotline
https://www.thehotline.org/
1-800-799-7233 (SAFE)

APPENDIX A: RESOURCES

National Sexual Assault Hotline
https://www.rainn.org/
1-800-656-4673 (HOPE)

POWER AND CONTROL WHEELS

DOMESTIC ABUSE INTERVENTION PROGRAMS
202 East Superior Street
Duluth, Minnesota 55802
218-722-2781
www.theduluthmodel.org

Understanding the Wheels
https://www.theduluthmodel.org/wheels/understanding-power-control-wheel/

Visit the Wheel Library for a variety of situations and languages.
https://www.theduluthmodel.org/wheel-gallery/

Appendix B: Church Policy Template and Checklist

APPENDIX B: CHURCH POLICY TEMPLATE AND CHECKLIST

Model Template for Creating a Church Policy

Domestic Violence Policy Template

(You may use this model policy as a template to create your own church policy.)

[Church Name] is committed to maintaining a safe environment for victims and survivors of abuse. **[Church Name]** believes that all forms of abuse are wrong and incompatible with Christian character. We affirm that all are one in Christ - equal before God in dignity, worth, and value.

Domestic violence is defined as a pattern of behavior used by one partner to gain and maintain power and control over the other partner. This includes not only physical assault, but also verbal, emotional, sexual, financial, digital/electronic, and spiritual abuse, as well as stalking. When a spouse is being abused, it is possible that the children are also at risk.

We will seek to:
    [Church Name] will protect those vulnerable to abuse from harm.
    Ensure that victims of abuse are connected to local resources.
    Provide support and assistance to victims, as needed.
    Speak of domestic violence from the pulpit, and in group discussions.
    Integrate conversation about healthy relationships in existing activities and groups.
    Create opportunities for survivors to share their experiences, if desired.

Our guidelines:
    [Church Name] will respect the autonomy of the victim.
    We will avoid blaming or shaming the victim, or minimizing the abuse.
    We will assure confidentiality (within the limits of mandated reporting).
    We will report to the police or civil authorities, if necessary.
    We will know our limitations, and seek professional assistance as needed.

Scheduled training:
    [Church Name] will hold (annual/biennial/other) trainings on the topic of abuse for staff/deacons/elders to ensure that all are educated on this topic.

Partnership with existing services:
    [Church Name] will establish/maintain a relationship with a local family violence shelter.
    We will network with local agencies who provide services for victims of abuse.
    We will have a contact list of referrals for victims who seek assistance.
    We will seek additional training on abuse from local resources who offer it.
    We will support local advocacy efforts regarding domestic violence.

Clergy Signatures Here

Used with permission by the Center for Church and Community Impact, at the Diana R. Garland School of Social Work, at Baylor University.

APPENDIX B: CHURCH POLICY TEMPLATE AND CHECKLIST

Suggested Checklist for Faith Leaders and Churches

- Know how to define abuse and what it looks like.
- Use trauma-informed, victim-centered responses to abuse.
- Learn about safety planning.
- Prioritize safety for victims of abuse.
- Assure confidentiality.
- Practice empathetic listening. Believe the victim.
- Do not blame or shame the victim.
- Affirm the victim's strength in seeking help.
- Communicate that God's heart is for the oppressed and that God cares about their pain.
- Know your state's mandated reporting laws.
- Understand and respect cultural differences.
- Be sensitive to marginalized individuals and groups.
- Resolve to eliminate abuse within your faith community.
- Have a plan for how to handle the one who perpetrated harm.
- Create procedures for handling abuse.
- Have a written policy on domestic violence.
- Discuss domestic violence in any premarital counseling sessions.
- Include the topic of abuse in sermons, including adding disclaimers about abuse when preaching and speaking about marriage and relationships.
- Refrain from using couples counseling in cases of abuse.
- Be familiar with your nearest family violence shelter.
- Display brochures about abuse around the church.
- Know your limitations and refer to specialized services as needed.

- Have a list of resources ready for victims and survivors of abuse.
- Offer space for survivor support groups, if possible.
- Place women in visible positions of leadership.
- Engage in continued training about abuse and trauma.
- Bring in guest speakers on the topic of domestic violence.
- Plan annual training for church staff, deacons, elders, and/or the entire congregation.

Appendix C: Premarital Counseling

THE EARLIER COUNSELING HAPPENS in the engagement period the better. If you meet with the couple for multiple sessions, consider meeting separately with each party for a session. Doing so would create time to discuss abuse with each of the individuals, but it is also a good practice to discuss abuse when they are in a session together, to be sure they are on the same page with intentions and expectations. Discuss topics like values, consent, addictions, pornography, anger, verbal harassment, expectations for intimacy, and financial control. Determine whether both individuals are entering into the conversation freely, but keep in mind that words do not always match the underlying attitudes and behaviors.

Consider asking if either partner experienced abuse in childhood or a prior relationship, keeping in mind that being a child victim of abuse is a predictor of being either a perpetrator or a victim as an adult. Determine if either partner brings in rigid gender-role expectations. Will there be mutual input and cooperation on financial decisions, household chores, and child-rearing?

Consider the vows the couple will exchange. Whether traditional or custom, there are ways that individuals can twist words later to effect harm in toxic or abusive marriages. For example, abusers may insist the vows contain words like *submit* and *obey* and will then use reminders of the vows to keep a victim in line. Discuss how vows ought to reflect equality and mutuality.

APPENDIX C: PREMARITAL COUNSELING

Consider discussing with them the Power and Control Wheel and the Equality Wheel. This is a good way to launch a discussion of fairness and beneficial, two-way respect in a relationship. Place a focus on appropriate spousal attitudes and behavior toward each other. Appendix A provides more information about the wheels.

Be clear with the couple that any abusive behavior breaks the marriage covenant. The victimized spouse is not bound to a destructive marriage. If the victimized spouse is willing to stay and work on the relationship, recommend professional individual counseling for both parties. Remember that couples counseling is contraindicated in cases of abuse. Provide support to the one harmed, stating that you believe them and are ready to help. Seek to hold the abusive partner accountable for harmful actions. Use appendix D to recognize signs of abuse, and appendix E to assess change in a perpetrator over time.

Know that someone experiencing abuse at this stage (engagement and premarital counseling) may not understand or describe it as abuse. Some may question the occasional confusion or difficulty of the relationship, dismissing it in calmer times. Their homes of origin or faith background may cause them to believe that what they are experiencing is normal, or that they cannot leave an abusive relationship. Some may be determined that they can save a rocky relationship or fix a partner through love and submission. In these cases, if abuse comes to light after the wedding, you will need to be ready to offer support and pastoral care. The victim will need to know about forms of abuse, safety planning, community resources, and the importance of professional, trauma-informed therapy. Discussing abuse during premarital counseling may feel uncomfortable, but the importance of these discussions outweighs potential discomfort.

Appendix D: Ways to Recognize Abuse

IF THERE IS SOMETHING concerning or suspicious, take time to inquire. Do not discredit a victim just because the partner seems perfect at church. Do not assume that depression and fear are a sign of spiritual weakness or lack of faith. Take time to get to know the situation and potential victim (and children) when you think that abuse may be present in a relationship.

- Signs of injury, physical evidence of violence
- Injuries with suspicious and unconvincing explanations
- Mentions threats of harm
- Changes in clothing/hairstyles that may hide bruises or physical injury
- Conduct changes; moody, tense, jittery, nervous, or fearful
- Meek, subdued, passive, avoidant, or anxious behavior
- Seems sleep deprived, listless, fatigued, and ill
- Low self-esteem, depression
- Withdrawal from, or lack of participation in, formerly enjoyed activities
- Frequent absence or tardiness
- Reserved and distant, excessive need for privacy

APPENDIX D: WAYS TO RECOGNIZE ABUSE

- Overly apologetic and seems to personally feel at fault for everything
- Minimizes or denies abuse or excuses possible signs of abuse
- Makes excuses for partner's behavior
- Cannot disagree with their spouse
- Must check in excessively and get permission for everything
- Goes along with everything the partner says or does
- Worried about pleasing or angering their partner
- Avoids certain topics
- Limited access to money, phone, or transportation
- Fear of outside intervention
- Worry about retaliation
- Descriptions of "difficult" or "hard" marriage
- Belongings and property destroyed
- Fear of going home, fear of people in the home
- Uses Scripture or spiritual concepts to explain the marriage or behavior
- Mentions cameras, GPS trackers, or other methods of surveillance
- Isolation, frequent moving, doesn't have local friends/family/support
- Lack of food, proper shelter, heat/AC, or transportation; signs of neglect
- Poor hygiene; in need of clothing, medical/dental care, medication, or glasses

APPENDIX D: WAYS TO RECOGNIZE ABUSE

Forms of Abuse List

Have any of these been directed at you, one of your children, or an elderly family member?

- ☐ **Physical** – hitting/slapping; pushing; pulling hair; strangulation/choking; damaging property; throwing things; use of weapons; driving recklessly; sleep deprivation; restraint; forced drug/alcohol use; harming/threatening to harm pets.

- ☐ **Emotional/psychological** – intimidation; manipulation; dominance; blackmail; shame; taunting; ridicule; anger; jealousy; gaslighting; creating fear of harm; accusations of cheating; public embarrassment; controlling major decisions; isolation; eliminating systems of support.

- ☐ **Verbal** – yelling; screaming; swearing; name-calling; insults; criticism; lecturing; belittling accomplishments; threats to you or others.

- ☐ **Sexual** – manipulation into acts you are not comfortable with; unwanted touching; demanding sex after other forms of abuse; sexual assault; forced sex; rape; forced pregnancy or abortion; forced porn use; trafficking or forced prostitution.

- ☐ **Economic/financial** – control of finances; not allowing you access to money; not allowing or forcing work; harassment at work; not including you on accounts/car/house; using family finances on gambling or running up debts; destroying your credit.

- ☐ **Digital/electronic** – excessive calling/texting to harass or control you; using technology to track or monitor; requiring passwords; oversight of online activity; revenge porn.

- ☐ **Spiritual/religious** – using religious ideology to control you; forcing gender role expectations as a spouse or in the home; twisting scripture; using religion to guilt or shame; religious penalties; not allowing or forcing a particular church; using faith leaders against you.

- ☐ **Neglect** – silent treatment; refusing to take responsibility; abandoning you in an unknown place; not supplying adequate medical/dental/mental health care; not providing a safe home environment; never offering approval; withholding affection.

- ☐ **Stalking** – you are monitored through cameras, recording apps, spyware, smart home features, GPS locators, or other people; you are followed and harassed; you receive repeated unwanted attention, gifts, threats, or communication; these activities cause emotional distress or fear for safety.

Additional questions:

- Has your partner ever strangled/choked you?
- Are there guns, knives, or other weapons in your home?
- Do you feel unsafe in your home?
- Have you recently separated, or have you talked of doing so?
- Do you feel obligated to continuously forgive, forget, submit, and respect your partner without receiving the same in return?

Used with permission. For more information about abuse, please visit HopeRiseThrive.com.

Appendix E: How to Assess Change in Perpetrators

IT IS UNDERSTANDABLE THAT faith leaders would want to see a marked change in perpetrators. It can be easy to assume change has occurred without waiting to see whether actions match verbal declarations of change. True transformation takes years and requires an incredible amount of work on the part of the one who has perpetrated harm. A person who is truly repentant will exhibit humility, have a teachable spirit, and be willing to abide by such a list as the one below. The word *spouse* below indicates the victimized spouse but is understood to be a former spouse if separation and/or divorce occurs.

- Admits to causing harm and takes complete responsibility; does not blame the spouse or children in any way; does not make excuses; does not minimize or deny the harm; describes this behavior as abusive and against God's design for family relationships

- Does not seek to denigrate the spouse to others in the church, family, friend groups, workplaces, and anywhere the spouse interacts; uses no accusations, shows no bitterness, and is not demanding; does not separate the spouse from systems of support or turn those systems of support against the spouse

- Understands that abuse damages relationships with the spouse and children, sometimes irreparably; understands that can include damage to relationships with extended family, friends, and faith communities; understands that the abuse damaged the relationships and not the response of the spouse and children

- Respects the boundaries of the spouse and children; does not seek to be involved where there could be conflict; does not attend events where a presence could be triggering or remains at a safe distance away from the victims; does not remain in friend, family, church groups, and networks where the victimized spouse finds and receives support; chooses instead to find new support networks and accountability partners; does not display any ulterior motives or agenda

- Is willing to get help, including batterer's intervention programs, AA, NA, sexual addiction/porn programs, and professional therapy (the programs utilized should address the thoughts, attitudes, and actions of the person who has caused harm and seek new ways of relating to others); understands there is a connection between pornography use and infidelity and that it is damaging, misogynistic, and exploitative; does not state that any affairs, drug/alcohol use, and/or abusive acts were the fault of the victim

- Abides by protective orders without complaint; engages in no surveillance, stalking, tracking/monitoring, or harassment of the spouse and children; safely surrenders weapons to the proper authorities; agrees to terms of nonviolence

- Ceases from using Scripture and religious ideology to intimidate, coerce, manipulate, or guilt the spouse or children; does not attempt to force forgiveness and reconciliation; does not seek to turn clergy members or church leaders against the spouse and children

- Understands that God hates abuse and that divorce for abusive behavior is an acceptable end to a traumatic marriage; understands that all abusive behavior breaks and abandons the marriage vows made before God and that the oppressed spouse is not bound to a destructive marriage; if the spouse chooses to divorce, there is no retribution; if the spouse chooses to separate for a time, there is patience without any pressure for reconciliation while the spouse prays about the decision and receives counseling; continues to work on personal improvement through extensive professional counseling, even if the marriage cannot be restored

- Does not neglect the duties of a parent; pays all child support on time, willingly, and without complaint; pays for all court-ordered expenses such as health insurance, medical appointments, school-related and extra-curricular activities, and trauma-informed therapy for the children; does not dictate or control the therapists, doctors, or caregivers for the children; allows the other parent the right of first refusal when unable to care for the children during custody or visitation; is respectful in communication with the other parent, using the appropriate, agreed-upon channels for communication; does not speak badly of the other parent to the children; does not use the children as a tool of manipulation

- Does not challenge any supervised visitation; never uses the words "parental alienation" but instead takes responsibility for the behavior that caused any feelings of distrust and uneasiness in the children; respects boundaries and preferred methods of communication while the children heal, knowing it takes time to rebuild trust and establish new, healthy patterns of communication; does not engage in numerous unnecessary court filings.

- Respects the autonomy and agency of the spouse and children to make informed decisions for their own lives; does not use anger, intimidation, manipulation, or third-party interventions to control them; does not insist on personal preferences in the lives of the survivors who are seeking to recover after the trauma of abuse

- Is willing to be transparent regarding counseling, child support, court orders, intervention programs, weapons, etc. so that efforts and progress are clear; puts in years of time and attention to the details mentioned above; understands that establishing and maintaining new patterns of thought and behavior take time and intentionality; displays true repentance through ongoing effort, consistent self-examination, and comprehensive change

Bibliography

Bancroft, Lundy. *Why Does He Do That? Inside the Minds of Angry and Controlling Men*. New York: Penguin, 2002.

Barr, Beth Allison. *The Making of Biblical Womanhood: How the Subjugation of Women Became Gospel Truth*. Grand Rapids: Brazos, 2021.

Baskerville, G. "Is It Always Best to 'Stay for the Kids'? No, Not If the Home Is Toxic." Life-Saving Divorce, Sept. 27, 2020. https://lifesavingdivorce.com/abuse-and-kids/.

———. "What Was the Puritan View of Divorce?" Life-Saving Divorce, Dec. 19, 2020. https://lifesavingdivorce.com/puritanviewdivorce/.

CDC. "About Child Abuse and Neglect." CDC, May 31, 2022. https://www.cdc.gov/child-abuse-neglect/about/?CDC_AAref_Val=https://www.cdc.gov/violenceprevention/childabuseandneglect/fastfact.html.

———. "About Intimate Partner Violence." CDC, 2022. https://www.cdc.gov/intimate-partner-violence/about/.

Chaves, Mark, et al. *Congregations in 21st Century America*. Durham, NC: Duke University, Department of Sociology. National Congregations Study. 2021. https://sites.duke.edu/ncsweb/files/2022/02/NCSIV_Report_Web_FINAL2.pdf.

Coe, Hannah. "Act Justly: To Put Away and Save." Sermon at Calvary Baptist Church, Waco, TX, June 25, 2023.

Collins, Natalie. *Out of Control: Couples, Conflict and the Capacity for Change*. London: SPCK, 2019. Kindle.

De Vries, Wilco. "The Danger of Forcing Forgiveness." *Christianity Today*, Apr. 19, 2023. https://www.christianitytoday.com/ct/2023/mayjune/abuse-victims-danger-of-forced-forgiveness.html.

Dichter, Melissa E., et al. "Coercive Control in Intimate Partner Violence: Relationship with Women's Experience of Violence, Use of Violence, and Danger." *Psychology of Violence* 8 (2018) 596–604. https://doi.org/10.1037/vio0000158.

Domestic Abuse Intervention Programs. "Understanding the Power and Control Wheel." Domestic Abuse Intervention Programs, n.d. https://www.theduluthmodel.org/wheels/faqs-about-the-wheels/.

BIBLIOGRAPHY

———. "Wheel Information Center." Domestic Abuse Intervention Programs, n.d. https://www.theduluthmodel.org/wheels/.

———. "Wheel Library." Domestic Abuse Intervention Programs, n.d. https://www.theduluthmodel.org/wheel-gallery/.

Drumm, René, et al. "'God Just Brought Me through It': Spiritual Coping Strategies for Resilience among Intimate Partner Violence Survivors." *Clinical Social Work Journal* 42 (2014) 385–94. https://doi.org/10.1007/s10615-013-0449-y.

Fortune, Marie M. *Love Does No Harm*. New York: Continuum, 1995.

Goertzen, Geneece, and Caleb Fox. "Response of Christian Faith Leaders to Domestic Violence: Training, Beliefs, and Practice." *Journal of Religion and Spirituality in Social Work: Social Thought* 42 (2023) 431–57.

Goldstein, Barry. *The Quincy Solution: Stop Domestic Violence and Save $500 Billion*. Bandon, OR: Reed, 2014. Kindle.

Gregoire, Sheila Wray. *Rescuing and Reframing Common Evangelical Teachings about Sex and Marriage*. Vol. 1 of *Fixed It for You*. Self-published, 2023. Kindle.

Hamby, Sherry, et al. "Children's Exposure to Intimate Partner Violence and Other Family Violence." *Juvenile Justice Bulletin*, Oct. 2011. https://www.ojp.gov/pdffiles1/ojjdp/232272.pdf.

Hernon, Jolene, and Dan Tompkins, eds. "Intimate Partner Homicide." *National Institute of Justice Journal* 250 (2003). https://doi.org/10.1037/e569102006-001.

Holsomback, S. "Experience of Harm Assessment." Santolina Consulting, 2023. https://santolinaconsulting.com/resources/.

Homiak, Katie Brennan, and Jon E Singletary. "Family Violence in Congregations: An Exploratory Study of Clergy's Needs." *Social Work and Christianity* 34 (2007) 18–46.

Hotline, The. "Domestic Violence Statistics." National Domestic Violence Hotline, n.d. https://www.thehotline.org/stakeholders/domestic-violence-statistics/.

———. "Understand Relationship Abuse." National Domestic Violence Hotline, n.d. https://www.thehotline.org/identify-abuse/understand-relationship-abuse/.

Houston-Kolnik, Jaclyn D., et al. "Overcoming the 'Holy Hush': A Qualitative Examination of Protestant Christian Leaders' Responses to Intimate Partner Violence." *American Journal of Community Psychology* 63 (2019) 135–52. https://doi.org/10.1002/ajcp.12278.

Institute on Strangulation Prevention. *Let's Create Your Safety Plan*. Alliance for Hope International, Oct. 2021. https://www.familyjusticecenter.org/wp-content/uploads/2021/10/Safety-Plan-Brochure-Gen.pdf.

Leemis, Ruth W., et al. *National Intimate Partner and Sexual Violence Survey: 2016/2017 Report*. Atlanta: National Center for Injury Prevention and Control, Centers for Disease Control and Prevention, 2022.

BIBLIOGRAPHY

Lifeway Research. *Domestic and Gender-Based Violence: Pastors' Attitudes and Actions*. Lifeway Research, 2018. http://research.lifeway.com/wp-content/uploads/2018/09/Domestic-Violence-Research-Report.pdf.

Martin, Brian F. "This April, Let's Talk about the Critical Link between Child Abuse and CDV . . . and the Program That Can Curb Both!" Childhood Domestic Violence Association, Mar 31, 2019. https://cdv.org/2019/03/mistaken-for-physical-child-abuse/.

McMullin, Steve, et al. "When Violence Hits the Religious Home: Raising Awareness about Domestic Violence in Seminaries and amongst Religious Leaders." *Journal of Pastoral Care and Counseling* 69 (2015) 113–24. https://doi.org/10.1177/1542305015586776.

Meier, Joan S., and Sean Dickson. "Mapping Gender: Shedding Empirical Light on Family Courts' Treatment of Cases Involving Abuse and Alienation." *Law & Inequality* 35 (2017) 311–34. https://doi.org/10.2139/ssrn.2999906.

Mend Project, The. "Overt vs. Covert Behavior." The Mend Project, n.d. https://themendproject.com/overt-vs-covert-behavior-examples/.

Messing, Jill Theresa, et al. "Intimate Partner Violence and Women's Experiences of Grief: Intimate Partner Violence and Grief." *Child and Family Social Work* 20 (2015) 30–39. https://doi.org/10.1111/cfs.12051.

Miller, Susan L. *Journeys: Resilience and Growth for Survivors of Intimate Partner Violence*. Gender and Justice 5. Berkeley: University of California Press, 2018. Kindle.

Modi, Monica N., et al. "The Role of Violence against Women Act in Addressing Intimate Partner Violence: A Public Health Issue." *Journal of Women's Health* 23 (2014) 253–59. https://doi.org/10.1089/jwh.2013.4387.

Moulding, Nicole, et al. "Rethinking Women's Mental Health after Intimate Partner Violence." *Violence against Women* 27 (2021) 1064–90. https://doi.org/10.1177/1077801220921937.

Myhill, Andy. "Measuring Coercive Control: What Can We Learn from National Population Surveys?" *Violence against Women* 21 (2015) 355–75. https://doi.org/10.1177/1077801214568032.

Nash, Shondrah Tarrezz. "The Changing of the Gods: Abused Christian Wives and Their Hermeneutic Revision of Gender, Power, and Spousal Conduct." *Qualitative Sociology* 29 (2006) 195–209. https://doi.org/10.1007/s11133-006-9018-9.

Nason-Clark, Nancy, et al. *Religion and Intimate Partner Violence: Understanding the Challenges and Proposing Solutions*. Interpersonal Violence Series. New York: Oxford University Press, 2018.

NCADV. "Domestic Violence and Firearms." NCADV, Dec. 20, 2016. https://ncadv.org/blog/posts/domestic-violence-and-firearms.

———. "Statistics." NCADV, n.d. https://ncadv.org/statistics.

National Coalition for the Homeless. "Domestic Violence and Homelessness." National Coalition for the Homeless, 2009. https://nationalhomeless.org/domestic-violence/.

Office on Drugs and Crime. "Home, the Most Dangerous Place for Women, with Majority of Female Homicide Victims Worldwide Killed by Partners or Family, UNODC Study Says." United Nations, Nov. 25, 2018. https://www.unodc.org/unodc/en/frontpage/2018/November/home-the-most-dangerous-place-for-women-with-majority-of-female-homicide-victims-worldwide-killed-by-partners-or-family--unodc-study-says.html.

Office on Women's Health. "Effects of Domestic Violence on Children." US Department of Health and Human Services, Feb. 15, 2021. https://www.womenshealth.gov/relationships-and-safety/domestic-violence/effects-domestic-violence-children.

Payne, Philip B. *The Bible vs. Biblical Womanhood: How God's Word Consistently Affirms Gender Equality*. Grand Rapids: Zondervan, 2023. Kindle.

Perilla, Julia L. "The Role of Churches in Preventing Domestic Violence: Can Churches Really Do Anything about Domestic Violence?" Catholic News Service, 2006. Website discontinued.

Philips, Allie. "Understanding the Link between Violence to Animals and People." ASPCA, 2014. https://nationallinkcoalition.org/wp-content/uploads/2014/06/Allies-Link-Monograph-2014.pdf.

Postmus, Judy L., et al. "Understanding Economic Abuse in the Lives of Survivors." *Journal of Interpersonal Violence* 27 (2012) 411–30. https://doi.org/10.1177/0886260511421669.

Reaves, Brian A. *Police Response to Domestic Violence, 2006–2015*. Bureau of Justice Statistics Special Report, May 2017. https://bjs.ojp.gov/content/pub/pdf/prdv0615.pdf.

Resource Center on Domestic Violence: Child Protection and Custody. "Co-Occurrence of Child Abuse and Domestic Violence Exposure." National Council of Juvenile and Family Court Judges, n.d. https://www.rcdvcpc.org/co-occurrence-of-child-abuse-and-domestic-violence-exposure.html.

Rotunda, Rob J., et al. "Clergy Response to Domestic Violence: A Preliminary Survey of Clergy Members, Victims, and Batterers." *Pastoral Psychology* 52 (2004) 353–65. https://doi.org/10.1023/B:PASP.0000016939.21284.a3.

Shannon-Lewy, Colleen, and Valerie T. Dull. "The Response of Christian Clergy to Domestic Violence: Help or Hindrance?" *Aggression and Violent Behavior* 10 (2005) 647–59. https://doi.org/10.1016/j.avb.2005.02.004.

Shellnutt, Kate. "Grace Community Church Rejected Elder's Calls to 'Do Justice' in Abuse Case." *Christianity Today*, Feb. 9, 2023. https://www.christianitytoday.com/news/2023/february/grace-community-church-elder-biblical-counseling-abuse.html.

Shinde, Avantica. "Black Women, Police Brutality, and the Violence against Women Act: How Pro-Arrest Policies Facilitate Racialized and Gendered Police Violence." *Georgetown Journal of Gender and the Law* 22 (2021) 1–2. https://www.law.georgetown.edu/gender-journal/online/volume-xxii-online/black-women-police-brutality-and-the-violence-against-women-

act-how-pro-arrest-policies-facilitate-racialized-and-gendered-police-violence/.
Simonič, Barbara. "The Power of Women's Faith in Coping with Intimate Partner Violence: Systematic Literature Review." *Journal of Religion and Health* 60 (2021) 4278–95. https://doi.org/10.1007/s10943-021-01222-9.
Smith, Sharon G., et al. "Intimate Partner Homicide and Corollary Victims in 16 States: National Violent Death Reporting System, 2003–2009." *American Journal of Public Health* 104 (2014) 461–66. https://doi.org/10.2105/AJPH.2013.301582.
Sokoloff, Natalie J., ed. *Domestic Violence at the Margins: Readings on Race, Class, Gender, and Culture*. New Brunswick, NJ: Rutgers University Press, 2005.
Stankorb, Sarah. "Inside the Church That Preaches 'Wives Need to Be Led with a Firm Hand.'" Vice, Sept. 28, 2021. https://www.vice.com/en/article/m7ezwx/inside-the-church-that-preaches-wives-need-to-be-led-with-a-firm-hand.
Thomas, Dorothy Q., and Michele E. Beasley. "Domestic Violence as a Human Rights Issue." *Human Rights Quarterly* 15 (1993) 36–62. https://doi.org/10.2307/762650.
Tracy, Steven R. "Clergy Responses to Domestic Violence." *Priscilla Papers* 21 (2007) 9–16.
———. "Domestic Violence in the Church and Redemptive Suffering in 1 Peter." *Calvin Theological Journal* 41 (2006) 279–96.
UN News. "A Staggering One-in-Three Women, Experience Physical, Sexual Abuse." United Nations, Nov. 24, 2019. https://news.un.org/en/story/2019/11/1052041.
Walker, Lenore. *The Battered Woman*. New York: HarperCollins, 1979. Kindle.
Wallace, Maeve E. "Trends in Pregnancy-Associated Homicide, United States, 2020." *American Journal of Public Health* 112 (2022) 1333–36. https://doi.org/10.2105/AJPH.2022.306937.
Westenberg, Leonie. "'When She Calls for Help'—Domestic Violence in Christian Families." *Social Sciences (Basel)* 6 (2017) 1–10. https://doi.org/10.3390/socsci6030071.
Wiesel, Elie. "Nobel Prize Speech." Elie Wiesel Foundation for Humanity, n.d. https://eliewieselfoundation.org/about-elie-wiesel/nobel-prize-speech/.
Zolotor, Adam J., et al. "Intimate Partner Violence and Child Maltreatment: Overlapping Risk." *Brief Treatment and Crisis Intervention* 7 (2007) 305–21. https://doi.org/10.1093/brief-treatment/mhm021.
Zust, Barbara, et al. "10-Year Study of Christian Church Support for Domestic Violence Victims: 2005–2015." *Journal of Interpersonal Violence* 36 (2021) 1856–82. https://doi.org/10.1177/0886260518754473.
Zust, Barbara L., et al. "Evangelical Christian Pastors' Lived Experience of Counseling Victims/Survivors of Domestic Violence." *Pastoral Psychology* 66 (2017) 675–87. https://doi.org/10.1007/s11089-017-0781-1.

www.ingramcontent.com/pod-product-compliance
Lightning Source LLC
Chambersburg PA
CBHW030114170426
43198CB00009B/622